The Social Teaching of the Black Churches

The Social Teaching of the Black Churches

Peter J. Paris

FORTRESS PRESS **Philadelphia**

Chapters 1 and 2 are revisions of two lectures published in *The Drew Gateway* 52 (Spring 1982), 1–38, and are used by permission.

Library of Congress Cataloging in Publication Data

Paris, Peter J., 1933–
    The social teaching of the Black Churches.

    Bibliography: p.
    Includes index.
    1. Afro-American churches.   2. Afro-Americans—
Religion.   3. Sociology, Christian—United States.
    I. Title.
    BR563.N4P37 1985   261.8′08996073   84–47930
    ISBN 0–8006–1805–X (pbk.)

K973G84   Printed in the United States of America   1–1805

For my mother,
    Violet Agatha Jewell Paris,
        who lives in the black Christian tradition;
and to the memory of
    my father, Freeman Archibald Paris, 1910–1972;
    and my sister, Mary Magdalene Paris, 1934–1971,
        who lived and died in the black Christian tradition

Contents

Acknowledgments

The conceptual framework for this study emerged gradually after a long period of painstaking reading of official denominational documents of the black Baptist conventions and Methodist conferences. Such an investigation was undertaken as a means of getting in tune with the thought and ethos of those denominations by attending to their own records. I have always felt a certain kinship with the independent black churches in the United States in spite of the fact that my early life had been nurtured in an Eastern Canadian black church tradition that had much less autonomy than its counterpart in this country. That spirit of kinship, more than anything else, has motivated me to probe the depth dimensions of these denominations in order to discover their essence, that is, that which distinguishes them from white denominations and designates their uniqueness.

This project could not have been brought to fruition apart from the assistance of many colleagues and associations, a few of which I will mention here. The principle that I have called "the black Christian tradition" was first described in a lecture at the annual meeting of the Society of Christian Ethics in 1979 and later published in its Selected Papers under the title "The Social Teaching of the Black Churches: A Prolegomenon." Large portions of that essay appear in chapter 1 of this book. Similarly, a large portion of chapters 1 and 2 was presented in two lectures at a northeastern conference of black United Methodist ministers held at Drew University Theological School in April 1982. These lectures were published later under the title "The Social World of the Black Churches" in the Spring 1982 issue of *Drew Gateway*. In March 1982, chapter 2 was delivered as a public lecture to a seminar at Chicago Theological Seminary. In October 1982, an essay on the methodological assumptions and principles underlying this present work was presented to the Society for the Study of Black Religion at its annual meeting in Atlantic City. In the spring of 1983, the argument of chapter 5 was presented as a lecture at Lafayette College, and in October 1983 it received a further hearing at the meeting of the Society for the Study of Black Religion which was held in conjunction with the Centennial Celebration of Gammon Theological Seminary in Atlanta. Finally, the first full draft of the manuscript was read and discussed in the spring of 1983 by my students in a doctoral level constructive ethics seminar at Vanderbilt Divinity School. I have felt singularly honored to be associated with all of these events and have received much valued help from each of them.

I wish to thank my excellent colleagues Professor Howard Harrod and Daniel Patte of Vanderbilt Divinity School and Dean Thomas W. Ogletree of Drew University Theological School for reading the manuscript in its entirety and for offering many helpful suggestions and much encouragement. I am also grateful to my close friend and colleague, Kelly Miller Smith, who has helped me in more ways than words can express, and whom I consider to be an embodiment par excellence of the black Christian tradition.

I wish also to thank the Vanderbilt Research Council for awarding me a Summer Research Fellowship which enabled me to pursue this project in important ways.

Finally, my family association has been a primary source of encouragement for me in all my work, and especially in this project. Accordingly, I take no small amount of pleasure in thanking Shirley, Valerie Lynn, and Peter Brett for their devotion.

PETER J. PARIS
Vanderbilt University
Nashville, Tennessee

Introduction

This study offers a constructive interpretation in religious social ethics, based primarily on the official records of two selected black denominations that represent the oldest and most prominent institutional paradigms of Christianity in black America, namely, the African Methodist Episcopal Church and the National Baptist Convention, U.S.A., Inc. After considerable study we have concluded that the social teaching of other black denominations in the Methodist and Baptist traditions — for example, the African Methodist Episcopal Zion Church, the Christian Methodist Episcopal Church, the National Baptist Convention of America, and the National Progressive Baptist Convention — does not differ appreciably from that of our selection. Hence, for our purposes, the respective black Baptist and Methodist traditions are analyzed as if they comprised two institutions. Accordingly, very little attention is given to the organizational differences within either tradition.

Usually one assumes that a study of two denominations will lead to the discovery of considerable differences between them. This has not been our experience in this inquiry. On the contrary, we have discovered no distinctive differences in the social thought of the respective black Baptist and Methodist denominations. Further, since a similar plurality of perspectives exists within each, no adequate classification of the types of social teaching can be developed solely along denominational lines.

In this analysis particular importance is given to the presidential and episcopal addresses delivered at the Baptist conventions and Methodist conferences from the late nineteenth century to recent decades. Our rationale for limiting this work to official denominational records rests on the assumption that basic communal values are legitimated and preserved by a community's religious institutions. Accordingly, we contend that the official leaders of the latter express (either explicitly or implicitly) their community's most basic values in their public addresses, deeds, and actions. Thus, a presidential or an episcopal address is always, in large part, ritualistic in both form and substance. That is to say, such presentations represent the community's most basic values in a way that is readily identifiable to that community. In a sense, the subject matter for such addresses is the particular tradition in which the speaker stands. The task of the speaker is to give new life to that tradition without changing its substance. Thus, such events usually are void of novelty and are often considered mundane by those who desire institutional change. In general, the public discourse of religious leaders usually aims at preserving and reviving the substance of their respective traditions. Those who do otherwise risk alienation from their particular communities.

Let us hasten to add that this analysis should not be interpreted as one that is bent on ignoring the thought of those religious leaders who have sought to bring about some measure of institutional change in their respective denominations. As a matter of fact, we hold no special brief for any particular ideological position within the denominations. We are concerned only that the documents analyzed have some measure of official denominational status in order for us to make general claims about the churches and their social teaching. Further, we will argue that the black denominations have demonstrated immense capacity for the inclusion of a wide variety of perspectives within their purviews, and we will also describe the principle that limits their capacity for inclusion.

Since the black churches have had a peculiar place of institutional primacy in the black community, and since they have been the custodians of the black community's most basic societal values, we contend that any description of the ethics of black Americans must, first of all, set out to clarify those religious and moral values which function normatively in both the official statements of the churches and the public discourse of their most respected leaders. Second, any such analysis must show not only how those values determine the nature of good and evil for blacks but also how they designate the communal spirit of the people—that spirit which forms the basis for their collective experience of racial solidarity.

The purpose of this study is to describe the way in which those basic communal values culminate in a distinctive principle of coherence which forms the bedrock of black American religious existence. We have called that principle "the black Christian tradition" in order to indicate that it is not a mere formal concept but a constellation of religious and moral values preserved in institutions and expressed in speeches, deeds, and actions. Most important, this tradition designates the unique contribution of the black churches to the nation and the world. It designates the worldview of black Americans and is the principal criterion for their assessment of everything affecting their common life.

We argue that the basic values implied by this tradition represent (1) the primary cause for the emergence of the black independent churches of the nineteenth century and (2) the sustaining force for their life to the present day. Further, we show how those values have functioned in the internal life of the churches and their effect on all the efforts of the latter to enhance racial justice in the society at large. In accordance with a profound insight of W. E. B. DuBois, this inquiry demonstrates that the "double-consciousness" of black Americans has led the black churches to internalize an ambiguous social ethic that has served, on the one hand, as a lure toward an ideal vision of society and, on the other hand, as a serious restraint on the race's sociopolitical development. This moral conflict permeates all aspects of their common life, that is, their autonomy, moral agency, political orientation, and understanding of power. In short, the principal task of this study is to analyze the nature of those moral dilemmas in order to point out their implications for thought and action in the religious, moral, and political spheres of the black community.

Clearly, all scholars agree that the black American experience has been proscribed historically by structural conditions of societal injustice. Over three hundred years of slavery followed by another century of racial segregation and discrimination evidence that fact. But throughout that period the black churches have had a prominent role in shaping, maintaining, and enhancing social order and communal solidarity by what sociologists call "adaptive" and "expressive" functions. In addition, they have inculcated in their people fundamental moral responses to such conditions which, while varying in accordance with the intensity of the adversity encountered from one time to another, nevertheless comprised, then and now, the authoritative basis for moral existence in the black community.

This study rests on the assumption that the social cohesion of every society is based on a set of shared values that find significant expression in various communal symbols, ideas, rituals, and pronouncements. Those values constitute the paramount cultural paradigm in which the people find their sense of identity and solidarity. More important, however, that root paradigm constitutes the ultimate authority for all moral obligation, legal enactment, social organization, and political association. In fact, no social or political advocacy in the society can gain legitimacy apart from an appeal to that paradigm. Further, we argue that the black churches have always understood that paradigm to be grounded in the Judeo-Christian understanding of human society.

This constructive interpretation of the relationship of church and society in the black American experience seeks to explicate the elements of a black American religious social ethic. Once again, it is important to emphasize that these elements are not abstract moral principles but, instead, sociopolitical quests for liberation and freedom. Further, they seem to be always present in the speeches, deeds, and actions of black religious leaders who set them forth as real possibilities within their historical contexts.

It must be said, however, that this study differs from an older form of black scholarship that modeled itself methodologically after studies that sought solely to describe the impact of oppression on the oppressed. The results of such endeavors were predictable, namely, high levels of pathological disorder psychologically, socially, politically, and religiously. Obviously that type of scholarship prevented blacks from emerging in the literature as agents of constructive social change.

The recent rise of black liberation thought (James H. Cone represents the progenitor of this new method in black, religious research, and we are very much indebted to him for his pioneering works in this area) has occasioned the birth of a revisionist genre of scholarship by developing a new hermeneutic, namely, that of dealing with the experience of oppression from the perspective of the oppressed and evaluating the efforts of the latter to liberate themselves. This genre has assumed a high measure of cognitive, moral, religious, social, and political agency on the part of the oppressed in spite of their crippling environmental conditions. This method has also rejected all philosophies of history that presuppose a generic understanding of human thought and action. In fact, it has radicalized the notion that all perspectives are grounded in specific sociocultural experiences. The result of this new approach has been liberating for all the oppressed because it validates their experience by relativizing the perspectives of their oppressors. Thus, it enables oppressed peoples to be studied as agents rather than as mere victims. While our study is positively related to this nascent tradition, its distinctive contribution lies in our identification of the fundamental principle underlying the black religious experience and the way that principle has functioned in the black churches as both lure and constraint in the pursuit of racial justice. Unlike the black theology of James Cone and others, our hermeneutical principle emerges out of the historical materials of black religion rather than being applied from without. Unlike the concept of "black liberation theology," our principle is not alien to the black church tradition. Rather, the latter is replete with relevant antecedents depicting its nature and function. Moreover, since we have attempted to depart minimally from the language of its bearers, our principle is not likely to be greeted by the ambivalence they afforded black liberation theology.

This study is a critical, ethical analysis of the self-understanding of black denominations in the Baptist and Methodist traditions. Regarding the basic principle that justifies the origin and continued existence of those traditions, there is no discernible difference between the two. That is to say, differences of polity and distinctive historic doctrines depict their continuity with their white counterparts, but as black churches their fundamental distinction lies in the principle that we call "the black Christian tradition." In relation to that principle, the black denominations are united.

In chapter 1 we argue that a comprehensive understanding of black religion must include both its eschatological and its political dimensions in order to grasp the phenomenon of religion adequately. The nineteenth-century black church independence movement is discussed as an effort to institutionalize a nonracist principle grounded in a biblical anthropology, implying moral and political obligation for the society as a whole. In that surrogate world created by the black churches, these churches were able to experience both independence from the domination of racism and the freedom to speak and act in opposition to it.

In chapter 2 we describe two moral dilemmas that have been at the heart of the black churches. The first dilemma pertains to two conflicting loyalties that have always plagued black Americans: the one in relation to the nation, and the other in relation to the race. Regarding the first, blacks have always felt a dilemma between their commitment to the principles of the American Constitution and their resistance to America's widespread practice of racism. More than anything else, their loyalty to the Constitution has been the chief cause of their general resistance to revolution as either an aim or a strategy for social change. Similarly, the second dilemma comprises an ecclesiastical conflict between their loyalty to the idea of the one universal church, on the one hand, and their devotion to a racially separate church on the other.

After sketching a framework for a moral theory on the relationship of person and society, we describe in chapter 3 the nature of the moral conflict that permeates the moral agency of the black churches. Since these churches have always assumed that racial development must be viewed as a means to the realization of civil rights rather than as an end in itself, they have been constrained thereby in all areas of racial development. Consequently, the churches have not been able to overcome their vulnerability to the charge that concentrated effort toward racial development aims at racial self-sufficiency, which is the goal of those radical black organizations with which the black churches have had little or no association. This chapter also reveals the failure of the black churches to discern that a considerable amount of their thought and action has been shaped in accordance with the values of the larger white society.

Chapter 4 constitutes a criticism of the function of the so-called political idealism of the black churches and the way in which that understanding has hindered all concentrated efforts toward the realization of race goals as well as limited their independence in theological, ethical, and political thought. In this context the conflict between the dual purposes of the churches, namely, between racial self-development and social transformation, is explicated. Further, this chapter introduces the implied sociology that underlies the political and religious idealism of the churches and the way in which that sociology conflicts with the value of cultural pluralism that is becoming increasingly acceptable in the black community at the present time.

Chapter 5 presents the understanding of power that has guided the life of the black churches, that is, "communal power." In this chapter we attempt to describe the difference between the type of power that has governed the larger racist society and that which governs those who traditionally have understood themselves as social reformers rather than revolutionaries. We argue that the power of the former aims at the other's destruction while that of the latter may contribute to self-destruction. Both stand in need of communal power, which includes a capacity to produce an effect as well as the capacity to undergo an effect. Either of these in isolation from the other is destructive. Our presumption, nevertheless, is that blacks generally stand in a greater readiness to participate in communal relationships with whites than vice versa, because each has been shaped historically by differing understandings and experiences of power. In spite of the various problems associated with the differing understandings of power, we conclude that the problem of the twenty-first century in American race relations will be the quest for power by blacks — the quest that marked the beginning of this new era, which was made possible by the constitutional guarantees gained by the culminating activity of the civil rights movement under the leadership of Martin Luther King, Jr.

1

A Surrogate World

BLACK RELIGIOUS SCHOLARSHIP

Scholarly opinion regarding the relationship of the black church to the American society can be classified as compensatory[1] and political.[2] The former contends that black religion is basically an otherworldly preoccupation seeking relief from the cruel realities of historical existence, while the latter views it as a dynamic agency for social change. The one implies a passive disposition toward social injustice, while the other infers an attitude of vigorous resistance.[3]

Each of these views is based on an inadequate understanding of the nature of religion in general and of black American religion in particular. The basis for this judgment lies in our view that it is the essence of every religion to be related to history in two ways: (1) to espouse a positive view of some distant future which serves as a lure for its adherents; and (2) to exhibit the basic sociocultural forms and values relative to its specific location. The former designates an eschatological[4] vision of the final end of humankind, while the latter expresses the nature and meaning of historical experience. To deny either the former or the latter is to distort the nature of religion per se. Hence generalizations on the basis of the one dimension of religious experience at the expense of the other constitute the major error implicit in both of those efforts to classify the black churches according to compensatory and political understandings.

Those who hold the compensatory position view the black

church as a pathological institution bent on leading its adherents away from reality to some illusory and/or suprahistorical ideal, that is, toward a repudiation of history. Correspondingly, those who affirm the political classification *see* the black churches as basically secular in nature, since, in that view, religion is reduced to politics, and both eternity and the sacred are denied thereby. Thus, in company with Vittorio Lanternari and other historians of religion, we conclude that either classification in isolation of the other is inadequate.

> Probably there is no phenomenon which reflects more clearly than do the religious movements among oppressed peoples the contradictory, yet indissoluble, bond between current reality and future goals, between history and eschatology, which lies at the root of almost every major human experience.[5]

The ensuing argument is rooted in the observation that the black churches have always had a profound concern for the bitter and painful realities of black existence in America as well as an abiding hope in a bright and radiant future (eschaton) free from any form of racial injustice. The latter, hope, designates the locus of ultimate value where all people are in harmony with the transcendent, holy, and supreme God of the Judeo-Christian faith. Traditionally, the black churches have interpreted human life, including all of its suffering and pain, in accordance with that ultimate goal in which they have never lost faith. The convergence of that sacred principle with their efforts for improved temporal conditions reveals the integral relationship of religion and politics in the black churches.[6]

The primary aim of this study is to explore the nature of religious thought in the black churches in order to determine the distinctiveness of a religion that encourages, sustains, and promotes (in varying good ways) political action as a necessary corollary, that is, as an action aimed at the creation of a good public realm, the quality of which is judged by the extent to which all of its citizens have the experience of freedom and the necessary resources for the full actualization of their potentialities.

In our view, good political action is the subject matter of social ethics. When political action is set in motion by some religious agency and either inferred or justified by a theological foundation, we call it religious social ethics. Hence we might also say that the aim of this study is to explicate the nature of the religious social ethic of the black churches.

During the past two decades, black scholarship[7] has exhibited a revisionist character. This contrasts with earlier scholarship, which tended to focus primarily on the impact of severe environmental forces on the race. In spite of the usefulness of such studies, they nevertheless depicted the victimization of the race and wholly disregarded the way in which blacks have sought to change their environment. Since victimization implies a condition of passivity, acquiescence, and forced obedience, the "new breed" of scholars has been diligently demonstrating that blacks have functioned in every historical period as agents of change in spite of the extreme environmental constraints upon them. Their capacity to find alternative ways of thinking and acting in such situations evidences the tenacity and resiliency of the human spirit in encounter with life-threatening conditions. The preservation of the power to think and act, rather than merely obey and adapt, is necessary for the preservation of human life per se. Absolute victimization implies the complete destruction of such a capacity and hence a reduction of human life to a lower state. In this respect, our study stands in the revisionist genre of black scholarship as it aims at showing the active role of the black churches in helping their people maintain self-respect as human beings in the face of powerful social forces aimed at their destruction. But, as we will see, this analysis makes its own unique methodological contribution to black religious scholarship by identifying the fundamental principle by which the independent black churches came into being and critically evaluating its implications for the thought and action of the churches.

THE QUEST FOR INDEPENDENCE[8]

From the beginning of the nation's history up to the present day, the black American experience has been characterized by racism — a phenomenon that employs race as a proscriptive principle for denying rights and opportunities, that is, a principle of societal exclusion. The system of hereditary slavery as practiced in the United States for three centuries best illustrates the absolutization of that principle. Slavery established a societal condition wherein blacks inherited at birth a status that excluded them from all of the privileges normally associated with being human. Slaves and their unborn progeny constituted part of their owner's total property assets; no freedom, no liberty, no rights. In short, the logic of the system was based on the proposition that blacks were not fully a part of the human race, a view that frequently sought legitimation in both science and religion. On the one hand the abolition of slavery marked the end of its absolute status, while on the other, it occasioned the beginning of a new era in which the principle of racism was destined to achieve a new form in which to express itself — that of racial segregation and discrimination. The practices of discrimination had been experienced by several generations of "freemen" in the North prior to their becoming the model for the inimitable, universal Jim Crow system in the South which achieved ascendancy round the turn of the present century and held sway until the 1960s when it was eradicated from the social order by the civil rights movement under the courageous leadership of Martin Luther King, Jr. Since then, new embodiments of the principle have attempted to take shape around the social realities of segregated housing patterns, of ghettoization (including its social, psychological, and economic implications), the end of which may well be the development of a permanent racial underclass with predictable economic, political, and social consequences. As the experience of slavery clearly reveals, social systems that are shaped by the principle of racism aim at total human annihilation. In the process of achieving its aim, the impact of racism virtually ensures restrictive and crippling effects both on the race as a whole and on the personal development of its members. Yet there is ample proof to demonstrate that blacks have not been totally destroyed by the exercise of this cruel and treacherous principle. On the individual level many have been brought down to the lowest depths, both mentally and physically. But on the group level the race has persevered, and that fact evidences the capacity of human beings to transcend incredibly stringent and cruel forces in an effort to preserve their humanity. The imaginative power and creative skill depicted in the countless Negro spirituals manifest that transcendence. Ironically, the destiny of those songs has not been confined to the restrictive world of the slave but has become woven into the fabric of America's distinctive cultural contribution to the world. Emerging out of the spirit of an oppressed people, these songs tell the universal story of agony and pain, but not that alone. They also tell of the faith and hope of suffering souls. Through the activities of poetry, music, and song the slaves expressed and preserved their humanity amidst astounding odds. And those activities comprise some of the earliest forms of resistance to their hostile environment.

Although many slaves responded to their situation by running away whenever they had the opportunity, and although others rebelled in various ways, the vast majority had no other choice than to learn how to cope with their predicament. Like all entrapped human beings, they desired freedom — a place wherein they could make their own decisions and determine their own destinies. In other words, they longed for a place of refuge from racism which, for them, was and continues to be the paramount social evil. Although they would have preferred their own sovereignty (i.e., a world controlled by themselves rather than by an external racist society), they were forced to settle for something less. The possibility of forming their own religious institutions appeared to be the only real option in that respect.[9] So they acted on the desire to create a world of their own regardless of the many obvious constraints confronting them. At first they sought permission to gather on the plantation for prayer, singing, and preaching. It is worthy of note that any success the slaves had in gaining the approval of their masters to hold such meetings required both careful deliberations and skillful diplomacy in their negotiations. Yet the attainment of such a goal always implied a measure of transcendence (sometimes only temporary) over one set of social conditions which they hoped would lead eventually to a fuller freedom.

During the last quarter of the eighteenth and the first half of the nineteenth century, blacks were able to found independent churches, [10] an activity that constituted the first black independence movement in America. In the white churches not only had blacks perceived a deliberate distortion of the Christian gospel but they feared a loss of their own self-respect should they continue indefinitely in a proscribed form of association with whites. From slavery through the period of Reconstruction they resolved to find ways of separating themselves from the religious and moral corruption endemic in the white churches in order to gain a measure of independence wherein they might affirm their own humanity in the light of a nonracist appropriation of the Christian message. Thus racism functioned as a negative cause for the separate racial churches, while blacks themselves constituted the positive thrust for independence. Here was evidenced a voluntary principle at work in what soon became a visible and irrevocable movement.[11] Needless to say, the full implications of that movement were only dimly perceived by their white rulers. Those nascent black churches evidenced the cooperative action of slaves to build institutions and prove to themselves and others that they were capable not only of adapting to an environment but of constructing a world of their own. In time, the black churches were destined to become a surrogate world for black people in general. While the larger society sought to victimize blacks, the black churches aimed at socializing their members into creative forms of coping along with the development of imaginative styles of social and political protest, both grounded in a religious hope for an eschatological victory.

The growth of the black churches is both significant and inspirational. In its history lie the stories of countless men and women, often slaves and runaway slaves, frequently freed men of humble economic stature, completely lacking in social status. Under paralyzing conditions, both during and after slavery, a multiplicity of black churches emerged, some on the plantations, others in segregated urban centers, many along the back roads in rural areas. In each case the black church was the primary community institution owned and controlled by blacks themselves.

Historically the churches have performed the many and varied functions of governance within the black community. The importance of those functions cannot be overemphasized. Constrained in every dimension of their common life by the dehumanizing conditions of white racism, blacks made their churches agencies for teaching the race how to respond to racial hostility in creative and constructive ways. E. Franklin Frazier has described the internal activities of the black churches as forms of compensation for the denial of freedom in the larger society. He viewed the churches as crucial social institutions for the maintenance and enhancement of civility, self-respect, social order, and communal belonging (identity). This institution was both broad and complex in its function and purpose. Frazier called this surrogate world "a nation within a nation":

> The Negro church was not only an arena of political life for the leaders of Negroes, it had a political meaning for the masses. Although they were denied the right to vote in the American community, within their churches, especially the Methodist churches, they could vote and engage in electing their officers. The election of bishops and other officers and representatives to conventions has been a serious activity for the masses of Negroes. But, in addition, the church had a political significance for the Negroes in a broader meaning of the term. The development of the Negro church after Emancipation was tied up, as we have seen, largely with the Negro family. A study of Negro churches in the Black Belt country in Georgia were "family churches." Outside of the family, the church represented the only other organized social existence. The rural Negro communities in the South were named after their churches. In fact, the Negro population in the rural South has been organized in "church communities" which represented their widest social orientation and the largest social groups in which they found an identification. Moreover, since the Negro was an outsider in the American community it was the church that enlisted his deepest loyalties. Therefore, it was more than an amusing incident to note some years ago in a rural community in Alabama, that a Negro when asked to identify the people in the adjoining community replied, "The nationality in there is Methodist." We must remember that these people have no historic traditions and language and sentiments to identify them as the various nationalities of Europe. For the Negro masses, in their social and moral isolation in American society, the Negro church community has been a nation within a nation.[12]

C. Eric Lincoln's conclusions about the relationship of the black church to the society are similar to Frazier's proposition that the compensatory and social protest views belong together because the "religious" and the "secular" are integrally connected in the black churches. He argues that there has always been an integral relationship between the black churches and the black community. In fact, he claims that among black Americans there is no radical disjunction between the sacred and the secular spheres of human existence. Rather, the cleavage that characterizes so much of Protestantism simply does not exist among black Americans.

> To understand the power of the Black Church it must first be understood that there is no disjunction between the Black Church and the Black community. The church is the spiritual face of the Black community, and whether one is a "church member" or not is beside the point in any assessment of the importance and meaning of the Black Church. . . . The Black Church, then, is in some sense a "universal church," claiming and representing all blacks out of a long tradition that looks back to the time when there was only the Black Church to bear witness to "who" or "what" a man was as he stood at the bar of his community. The Church still accepts a broad-gauge responsibility for the Black community inside and outside its formal communion. No one can die "outside the Black Church" if he is Black. No matter how notorious one's life on earth, the Church claims its own at death — and with appropriate ceremony.[13]

Further, Lincoln argues a point that has been reiterated by several others and that has important implications for the relationship of religion, ethics, and politics. He concludes, "The church is still in an important sense the people, and . . . the church leaders are still the people's representatives."[14]

Thus the multifarious functions of the black church justify the claim that they have been the institutional center of the black community; the basic source of religious and moral values; diligent in protecting the community from the many and varied abuses of racism by comforting the wounded, restoring dignity to the demoralized, hope to the despairing and redirection to those bent on harboring attitudes of bitterness and hatred as well as those disposed to acts of violence; prudent in devising and implementing forms of protest against racial injustices. Black churches have advocated the support of black businesses, established and maintained educational institutions, strengthened family life, provided a perspective for assessing the moral quality of the nation, and been closely allied with countless civil rights organizations and all other activities aimed at racial improvement. In short, they have a long and impressive history of institutional primacy in a racially segregated situation.

In addition, we contend that the black churches have a unique history of being the single most important institutions embodying goals and purposes that pertain primarily to the welfare of black people. That uniqueness is significant because in America there have been no other enduring institutions with such purposes. Rather, white institutions have always aimed at the welfare of whites even when they have espoused causes that seemingly focus on the welfare of blacks. Alexis de Tocqueville perceived that fact nearly one hundred fifty years ago in his startling conclusion regarding the crucial question of abolitionism: "It is not for the good of the Negroes, but for that of the whites, that measures are taken to abolish slavery in the United States."[15]

Further, the uniqueness of the black churches is seen in the fact that they are (as the literature constantly asserts) unequivocally "race institutions." As we have said, racism and racial self-respect have been the two warring principles that caused the emergence of the black churches. While those churches have much in common with various churches of the economically underprivileged[16] and socially impoverished, and while they minister to the peculiar needs of the race and strive for various forms of social amelioration, they cannot be understood completely by an appeal to social and economic forces. The churches of the lower classes tend (over a period of time) to become middle-class churches and thus completely assimilated into the predominant values, customs, and practices of the so-called mainline churches. That has not been the case with the black churches. Regardless of their socio-economic class stratification, they never cease being black churches — on the one hand victimized by racism, while on the other embodying, nurturing, and promoting a radically different view of humanity which they consider to be theologically correct, biblically sound, and morally indisputable.

THE BLACK CHRISTIAN TRADITION AS PROPHETIC PRINCIPLE

The tradition that has always been normative for the black churches and the black community is not the so-called Western Christian tradition per se, although this tradition is an important source for blacks. More accurately, the normative tradition for blacks is that tradition governed by the principle of nonracism which we call the black Christian tradition. The fundamental principle of the black Christian tradition is depicted most adequately in the biblical doctrine of the parenthood of God and the kinship of all peoples—which is a version of the traditional sexist expression "the Fatherhood of God and the brotherhood of men."

The terms "Western" and "black" designate two different but very significant modifications of Christianity. Each signifies a specifically different sociopolitical context in which the Christian religion has been appropriated and shaped. Since religious experience is always conditioned in important ways by its sociopolitical context, it follows that significant differences in the latter imply corresponding differences in the former. Consequently, since the black churches were racially segregated from their white counterparts, it should not be surprising to discover the reflection of that reality in the religion of blacks as well as in that of whites. But one should not assume (as many have) that the pathological conditions of the black community are the only forces shaping social reality. Rather, the black Christian tradition constitutes a graphic denial of that assumption.

The black Christian tradition became institutionalized in the independent black churches.[17] Prior to their emergence, the desire and quest for freedom, together with their concomitant resistance to slavery and racism, had no enduring public form. The principle of freedom and equality of all persons under God is not an abstract idea but a normative condition of the black churches, wherein all who participate can experience its reality. That is to say, the institutionalization of this principle in the black churches reveals its empirical status.

It was out of the crucible of racial oppression, then, that the black Christian tradition emerged as a nonracist appropriation of the Christian faith. As such it represented the capacity of the human spirit to transcend the conditions of racism in both thought and practice. In addition, this tradition has been represented as a fundamental principle of criticism justifying and motivating all endeavors by blacks for survival and social transformation. Thus the black Christian tradition has exercised both priestly and prophetic functions: the former aiding and abetting the race in its capacity to endure the effects of racism, the latter utilizing all available means to effect religious and moral reform in the society at large.

The black Christian tradition stands in opposition to the Western Christian tradition as the latter has been represented in white American churches. The black Christian tradition has always been the source of inspiration for black churches in their persistent attempts to reveal the fundamental depths of racism — that racial segregation and discrimination (not to mention slavery) differ from many other social issues in that they are rooted in a worldview that is both morally and religiously false. Accordingly, the black churches have revealed the self-contradictory nature of the race problem. Their basic source of authority has been that to which they have been unreservedly committed, namely, a biblical anthropology which they believe strongly affirms the equality of all persons under God regardless of race or any other natural quality. This doctrine has been the essence of the black Christian tradition and the most fundamental requirement of its churches. Its discovery soon revealed to blacks the basic contradiction implicit in the religion of white Americans: the contradiction between this biblical understanding of humanity and the practices of the white churches. Ironically, the portrayal of this dilemma has always been the strongest weapon the black churches have had in their attempts to reform the white churches. In short, the black Christian tradition posited a fundamental moral and religious dilemma in the heart of white Christianity and, in fact, was born in opposition to that problem.

The moral and political significance of the black churches is derived from a common source of authority, the black Christian tradition. Here the thought and practice of religion, politics, and morality are integrally related. That is to say, the one always implies the other. Whenever religion, politics, and morality are isolated from one another, the tradition itself is severely threatened.[18] Whenever individuals or groups betray the basic principles of that tradition, whether by direct assault or by some insidious compromise, they threaten the black community's integrity, since the latter is linked intrinsically with the moral and political dimensions of the black Christian tradition. In other words, not only has the black Christian tradition been normative for the black churches, it has also been the basic principle of meaning for the entire black community.[19]

Regardless of the measure of success that betrayers of the black Christian tradition may achieve, they have never been able to gain full legitimacy within the black community. Those who compromise the tradition are received, at best, ambivalently, and, at worst, they become liable to the community's most opprobrious epithet, "Uncle Tom." Those who explicitly attack the tradition alienate themselves from the community.

Thus the moral and political character of the black churches is based on an authority that is not the controlled possession of the churches themselves. Rather, it transcends them as both lure and judge. In fact, the churches are either praised or blamed by the community at large in accordance with their faithfulness to that tradition. Those who betray the tradition not only violate their own religious principle of authority but become vulnerable to the charge of forsaking the community's trust. Faithfulness to the principle of human equality under God and its implied opposition to racism alone determine the integrity of the churches and their relationship to the black community.

Clearly, the black Christian tradition has been the lifeline of the black community. It alone has constituted the ground for their claims of humanity and, as such, has always placed blacks in opposition to the prevailing ethos of the larger American society. Apart from the tradition it is doubtful that blacks would have been able to survive the dehumanizing force of chattel slavery and its legacy of racial oppression. As a creative and critical principle, the black Christian tradition has stimulated the interests and shaped the pursuits of countless artists, scholars, religionists, reformers, and the like. Embodied in the community's primary institutions, that is, the churches, it has been the source of ultimate meaning for their varied social functions. Surely the end of racism would imply the beginning of a new era for the tradition — an era in which the biblical understanding of humanity would continue to be proclaimed by the black church as normative for all people, but the proclamation would issue from a different vantage point. That is to say, the validity of the basic principle of the black Christian tradition would not be altered by the removal of the experiential condition of racism, because blacks believe that the tradition itself is grounded in the truth of God, which is eternal. Hence it is no understatement to say that the thought and action of the black churches cannot be understood apart from this principle, which to the black churches is what the Protestant principle is to Protestantism, namely, a prophetic principle of criticism. For the black churches every aspect of history must be related to this tradition. That idea was definitely implied by the African Methodist Episcopal bishops when they asserted that only the full realization of this prophetic principle would designate the end of the mission of the black churches.

> Bishop Payne crystallized the sentiment of all the distinguished statesmen and churchmen when he said, "God our Father; Christ our Redeemer; Man our Brother." This is the official motto of the A.M.E. church, and her mission in the commonwealth of Christianity is to bring all denominations and races to acknowledge and practice the sentiments contained therein. When these sentiments are universal in theory and practice, then the mission of the distinctive colored organizations will cease.[20]

Such a sentiment expresses the universal disposition of the black churches both then and now.

IMPLICATIONS OF THE PRINCIPLE
FOR MORALITY, RELIGION,
AND POLITICS

First, let us consider the implications of this prophetic principle for morality. Clearly, those black churches which have been faithful to the black Christian tradition are moral institutions. Their raison d'être is inextricably tied to the function of opposing the beliefs and practices of racism by proclaiming the biblical view of humanity as they have appropriated it, that is, the equality of all persons under God. Thus their moral aim is theologically grounded. The doctrine of human equality under God is, for them, the final authority for all matters pertaining to faith, thought, and practice. In short, its function in the black experience is categorical, that is, it is unconditional, absolute, and universally applicable. Consequently, all action (religious or political) that is aimed at correcting the social injustice of racism is viewed as moral action. But there is an important modification. The black Christian tradition has tended in the main, though not always, to refrain from justifying any acts of violence against other human beings. This dominant strand of the tradition has always viewed violence as self-contradictory, as a logical deduction from the idea that all persons are equal under God. Consequently, the black churches have believed that such a high estimation of human nature is contradicted whenever human beings destroy one another, however righteous the cause might be. Further, blacks have always perceived that that which is gained by violence and the threat of violence must be maintained similarly. Such is the way of nations in both their conquests and defenses. Although the black churches have always known that the black community has been formed and controlled in all dimensions of its life by the application of violence and its threat, they have chosen both for reasons of principle and strategy to oppose those forces by alternative, nonviolent methods.[21] Under the norm of the black Christian tradition they have fostered opposition to racism that has been both vigorous and creative. Their forms of action have tended always to be life-protecting, life-enabling, life-respecting. In short, their opposition to racism has contributed to the creation and preservation of community not only among blacks but between blacks and whites. As we will see later, the other side of this position on violence has not been entirely absent from the tradition and has always had a latent presence (chiefly in the form of a veiled threat) even among those who have advocated publicly the religious and moral significance of nonviolence.

In regard to the significance of the prophetic principle for religion, the ubiquity of racism has had a prominent influence on the way in which the black churches have defined themselves. As we have seen, they came into being to embody and express the biblical understanding that all persons are equal under God. Throughout their institutional life that ideal has functioned as a norm in their experience, inspiring their imaginations and governing their thought and action. Further, loyalty to that norm has been the greatest source of their unity, since all have long agreed that racism is a profound evil that must be resisted in some form by every self-respecting human being.

Though there are many theological implications of these facts, two are of the greatest importance. First, the black churches, under the norm of the black Christian tradition, are characterized by their common quest for human freedom and justice, that is, the equality of all persons under God. Second, that aim implies a strong doctrine of sin in relation to the problem of racism. Yet it also implies a strong doctrine of virtue on the part of those who oppose racism, seen especially in the cultivation of the virtues of self-reliance, self-support, self-determination, and self-respect — virtues that Booker T. Washington capitalized on, though he was not their progenitor. These virtues constitute racial and moral virtues, the validity of which have never been disputed by blacks. This dialectic becomes more graphic when one views its respective empirical poles: (1) the empirical referent for the doctrine of sin is white racism (i.e., as practiced by white people and their institutions in the main), while (2) the empirical referent for the doctrine of virtue is black resistance to racism by black people and their institutions.[22] Consequently, black churches faithful to the norm of the black Christian tradition have no radical doctrine of sin[23] that readily implicates all people (white and black) in the same way. Rather, the thought of the black churches distinguishes the "sins" of black people from the "sin" of white racism, which is considered by far the most wretched. Though the doctrine of human equality under God implies that none—including blacks—are justified in their attempts to subordinate the humanity of others, its application to blacks is often obscured by the prevalence of white racism in all walks of life. Thus, although blacks are guilty of oppressing other blacks (rarely are they in positions of power over whites), the churches generally give their attention to the fact that all blacks are oppressed by the greater force of white racism, which is considered the greater evil and possibly the source of all sin.

Finally, it is politically significant that the black Christian tradition justifies all action that is in opposition to racism insofar as its quality is commensurate with its goal, that is, affirming and establishing the equality of all persons under God. In other words, means and ends must be integrally related. Clearly, the black Christian tradition puts forward a principle of opposition to racism that is merely formal. The nature of its content must be decided in every context and hence must vary—not in its moral quality but in its practical relevance. That is to say, while certain forms of protest may have been appropriate in one period, they may be viewed as inadequate in another time and place. The demands of justice and the substance that it seeks to embody must vary according to the possibilities afforded by specific situations and contexts. The task of striving to effect legal guarantees for the civil rights of blacks was regarded in earlier decades as the rightful preoccupation of the churches as well as others. But the facts of social change may render those former strategies inappropriate for our present time. Rather, given formal legal advances, the contemporary situation may demand the development, preservation, and enhancement of substantial power for blacks (social, economic, and political) in all dimensions of our common life. Like every situation, the present is characterized by its possibilities, which necessitate clarification, specification, and the utilization of many and varied skills for effective decision and action. Whenever they have had the vote, either during Reconstruction or in the modern period, churches faithful to the black Christian tradition have never wasted time in questioning the moral and religious value of political engagement, for example, running for elective office, campaigning, active party membership, lobbying, and the like. Rather, they have always measured the validity of such activities by reference to practical wisdom as guided by their norm. Those who have done otherwise have revealed thereby their alienation from that tradition.

Thus, nothing more important can be said of the black churches than that they represent the historical embodiment of a universally significant principle. That alone — an anthropological principle grounded in the biblical understanding of the nature of humanity and its relation to God[24] — constitutes their uniqueness in American religious history. All of the functions of the black churches are attempts to mediate this theologically grounded anthropological principle with the demands of the racial situation in every period of history. This has always constituted the mission of the black churches to the larger American society. The novelty of this phenomenon was accurately accented by Bishop R. R. Wright in his highly respected *Encyclopaedia of the African Methodist Episcopal Church*, in which he described the way in which Richard Allen's movement was much more important sociologically than theologically because, for the first time, the world saw the birth of a church not on the basis of some new theological propositions but solely on sociological grounds.

> Richard Allen brought forth something new. For 1800 years of Christian organization, most denominations and divisions of the Christian Church have been brought about on purely theological differences. But for the first time certainly in American history, there was a Christian denomination built entirely upon sociological grounds: to promote brotherhood and equality across racial lines. For Richard Allen and his followers made no protest against Methodist theology or polity. They accepted the twenty-nine (29) Articles of Religion, The Catechism of Faith, the General Rules, the Rules for Bands, the Orders of the Ministry, the general organization from pastors, local preachers, class leaders to bishops, the annual conferences, etc. They established the General Conference as the chief

authority, and put the same restrictions on the General Conference as the Methodist did. It was Richard Allen's interpretation of the "second great commandment" — "Thou shalt love thy neighbor as thyself" to mean "thou shalt give equality to black people"— that caused the organization of Richard Allen's AME Church. And this was the first time in the history of western Christianity that a church included in a practical way black people on terms of equality. And this makes Richard Allen one of the outstanding Christian statesmen of all times. Careful research into the development of Christian activity, in our New World fails to reveal a single outstanding leader that thought it necessary to include black people in Christian Church life on terms of equality. Not even Augustine, who was born in Africa, and became one of the great bishops in the church; nor Martin Luther, the great reformer, nor John Calvin, the great theologian of Protestantism, nor even our own John Wesley, the founder of Methodism, who lived among the slaves in Georgia, nor any great American churchman antedating Allen, advocated and implemented equality in the church.[25]

Contrary to Bishop Wright's understanding of the relationship of sociology and theology, we contend that the two have been integrally related in the principle underlying the black Christian tradition which, incidentally, provides stronger religious grounds for Bishop Wright's viewpoint. Thus, in our view, the theological grounding of this anthropological principle established its religious character while the anthropological focus specified its social relatedness. In other words, the black Christian tradition represents a formal union of the eschatological and the sociopolitical realms, never the one apart from the other. In summation, morality, religion, and politics are united whenever this formal principle is actualized in the thought and practice of those persons or institutions wherein racism has no reality.

Although the principle itself was not created by the black churches, its institutionalization in those bodies has been a unique phenomenon in America. In fact, the black churches appropriated an idea that had only an abstract rhetorical appearance in the white churches, and they made it the bedrock of their existence. By so doing, they claimed that they had grasped the essence of the Christian faith and rescued it from its archenemy, namely, white racism.

There is no clearer empirical reference to this principle than that provided by Bishop C. M. Tanner at the turn of the century when he attempted to answer the question, "Why, in short, have we the right to maintain a separate organization?"— a question that constantly plagued many black leaders because of their fear of being accused of practicing racism in reverse. Bishop Tanner gave the following response:

> First, we would state that it is not only because Allen was pulled off his knees one hundred years ago that we have the right to a separate organization today. Had this been all that we had as a difference, I for one, even today, would say "Let bygones be bygones, let us return to the mother church." But the difference between Allen and those at St. George's and between our Church and the churches of the other race today, is not in this incident of long ago but in a fundamental Christian principle: *The question of the substantial oneness and brotherhood of all men.* Allen saw, our oppressed forefathers saw, and we see today, that it is the policy of the churches to discriminate between their members on account of their color and conditions. They refused to judge men by their merits but made color and conditions a test of acceptance. Hence as the Pilgrim fathers left their home seeking freedom of worship in the New World, so Allen and his followers left the church in which they had been reared because the first right of every man — liberty — had been denied them.
>
> The church which Allen founded stands today not only as the result of the incident at St. George's, but as a living protest against distinction in the church of Jesus Christ on account of race or color. We hold, teach and practice that God is no respecter of persons. (Acts 10:34) This may be spoken of as the *distinctive note* of African Methodism.
>
> We claim God our Father, Christ our Redeemer, Man our brother. Wesley called the world his parish; we call the inhabitants thereof our brothers. While we hold and keep ever in its foremost place the Fatherhood of God and the redemptive work of Christ our Savior, we also hold and seize every opportunity to apply the great truth taught in the parable of the good Samaritan. We preach, stand for and practice the truth that all men the white, the red, the yellow, the brown, the black, are all and are to the same extent, our brothers. We claim that there is but one race in the sight of God, the human race, and the blackest and the whitest are brothers. This we strive to hold, not as a mere high sounding, general statement, but as a great truth of which we seek to make practical application at

every opportunity that presents itself. That some may refuse to recognize this common brotherhood, or make light of our attempt to teach and apply it, does not surprise or discourage us. We believe that our position is that of Jesus and the Bible, and are content to allow time to prove that in this, we were in the vanguard of the march of practical Christianity. No man is under any disadvantage in our church by reason of his race or color. He is judged only by his fitness and ability. So that we have white preachers in our pulpits and not a few white members in our pews.

With the spread of the Gospel among the different races and the advance of trade and commerce, bringing the ends of the earth to our very doors, this question of oneness of the human family is bound to become more and more urgent in its demand for a settlement. Either the darker races, who are vastly stronger than the white races numerically, are brothers or they are not. For one to admit it in words and deny it in practice is hypocrisy.

The question is even now pressing for an answer and professing Christians will be compelled to put their faith into practice. When that time comes we will not have a whole class discriminated against in the business, social and religious spheres. Men will be employed according to their ability, will be given social recognition according to their moral and intellectual worth, and color will no longer be the qualification for acceptable membership in Christ's Church, which he purchased with his own blood.

Our church has been on record for almost one hundred years as an advocate of this principle. Thus far her labors have been singularly blessed.[26]

Finally, as both cause and norm of the independent black churches, the black Christian tradition has been the ground of unity among them in spite of their lack of agreement regarding strategies for opposing racism. The principle, nevertheless, constitutes the basis for an associational theory, since it has guided and continues to guide intentionality, moral action (individually and collectively), religious organization, and public purpose. Finally, this principle is wholly adequate for understanding the nature of the black churches and their social thought.

NOTES

1. The two most prominent representatives of the compensatory view are Benjamin E. Mays and E. Franklin Frazier, whose respective works

The Negro's God as Reflected in His Literature (New York: Atheneum Publishers, 1968) and *The Negro Church in America* (New York: Schocken Books, 1964) have become classics in this regard. In fairness to both, it must be said that they were cognizant of the political function as well, but viewed it as indicative of a move away from the religious to the secular realm — a movement they correlated with upward socio-economic mobility.

2. The principal representatives of the political view are the following: Carter G. Woodson, *The History of the Negro Church* (Washington, D.C.: Associated Publishers, 1921); Joseph R. Washington, Jr., *Black Religion: The Negro and Christianity in the United States* (Boston: Beacon Press, 1963); Gayraud Wilmore, *Black Religion and Black Radicalism* (New York: Doubleday & Co., 1972); Miles Mark Fisher, *Negro Slave Songs in the United States* (New York: Citadel Press, 1969); E. U. Essien-Udom, *Black Nationalism: A Search for an Identity in America* (New York: Dell Publishing Co., 1965). It should be added that black liberation theology has had a similar understanding of the black churches.

3. It is important to note that Vincent Harding affirms each of these views as functions of the black church and also allows for the possibility of one or the other being adequate descriptions of the black church in one place or the other and in one period or another. See his essay "Religion and Resistance Among Antebellum Negroes," in *The Making of Black America: Essays in Negro Life and History*, edited by August Meier and Elliott Rudwick (New York: Atheneum Publishers, 1969), 1:180ff.

4. This writer considers the term "eschatological" to be a more accurate description of the theology of the black churches than "compensatory," since "compensatory" implies a pathological rather than a prophetic orientation to historical realities.

5. Vittorio Lanternari, *The Religions of the Oppressed: A Study of Modern Messianic Cults* (New York: Alfred A. Knopf, 1963), x.

6. This is made clear by James H. Cone repeatedly in his works, but nowhere more so than in his statement, "Black thought was largely eschatological and never abstract, but usually related to their struggle against earthly oppression." See his *God of the Oppressed* (New York: Seabury Press, 1975), 54ff.

7. It must be noted that this revisionist orientation has considerable continuity with a tradition that became somewhat muted since the depression — a tradition that included such scholars as W. E. B DuBois, Carter G. Woodson, and Kelly Miller, to mention only a few.

8. The word "independence" is used here because historically it was used so frequently in the black churches to typify the self-understanding of their quest. In the contemporary period, black scholars and others have adopted the term "liberation" to depict the same reality. Unfortunately,

however, the black churches continue to view the term "liberation" with a certain amount of suspicion. At any rate, it has not as yet become "their" term.

9. It is important to note that the spirit of the American Revolution, propelled by the ideas of the Enlightenment, stirred the imagination of many social reformers both in this country and overseas. One of the implications of this new spirit, together with the obvious inconsistency of blacks fighting for America's independence from Britain while they themselves were still slaves, was the demand on the part of many for the abolition of the slave trade and, in some places, of slavery itself. See John Hope Franklin, *From Slavery to Freedom* (New York: Alfred A. Knopf, 1947), chap. 10.

10. See Albert J. Raboteau, *Slave Religion: The "Invisible Institution" in the Antebellum South* (New York: Oxford University Press, 1978), chap. 4; also Woodson, *The History of the Negro Church*, chap. 4; Franklin, *From Slavery to Freedom*, 161ff.

11. This independence movement had its beginnings in the late eighteenth century when "freemen" in the North founded the African Methodist Episcopal Church and the African Methodist Episcopal Zion Church, both of which experienced rapid and phenomenal growth following emancipation. Utilizing the same model of independence, the Colored Primitive Baptists in America, the Colored Cumberland Presbyterian Church, the Colored Methodist Episcopal Church, and the National Baptist Convention represented a portion of that momentum.

12. Frazier, *The Negro Church in America*, 44.

13. C. Eric Lincoln, *The Black Church Since Frazier* (New York: Schocken Books, 1974), 115–16.

14. In recent years many black scholars have drawn heavily upon this idea as a way of correlating black American religion with the traditional religion of Africa. For example, in a mimeographed paper entitled "Our Heritage and Our Hope," delivered and circulated among the members of the Society for the Study of Black Religion at its annual meeting in Jamaica, West Indies, November 1976, Gayraud Wilmore wrote, "There is no essential discontinuity between Africa and Afro-America, between black culture and black religion, between the black church and the black community." See also Wilmore, *Black Religion and Black Radicalism*, chap. 1. Further, it appears to this writer that this idea elaborates what Gunnar Myrdal saw dimly several decades ago when he wrote, "It must never be forgotten that the Negro church *fundamentally is an* expression of the Negro community itself" *An American Dilemma* (New York: Harper & Brothers, 1944), 2:875; the idea permeates James Cone, *The Spirituals and the Blues* (New York: Seabury Press, 1972). Charles H. Long draws out the implications of this idea for interdisciplinary scholarship. He says that "the black church is and has been the locus of the black

community. If this is so, then it means that the church is the locus of the expression of black cultural life. Politics, art, business, and all other dimensions of the black community should thus find their expression as aspects of the religious experience of black folks." See his "Assessment and New Departures for a Study of Black Religion in the United States of America," in *Black Religious Scholarship: Reflection and Promise*, Addresses at the 10th Annual Meeting of the Society for the Study of Black Religion, New York City, October 22–24, 1981, 7–8.

15. Alexis de Tocqueville, *Democracy in America* (New York: Alfred A. Knopf, 1945), 1:375.

16. H. Richard Niebuhr presents a good discussion of this phenomenon in his *Social Sources of Denominationalism* (New York: World Publishing Co., 1972), 26–27. For a more detailed discussion of the impact of economic conditions on the black churches, see St. Clair Drake and Horace R. Cayton, *Black Metropolis: A Study of Negro Life in a Northern City* (New York: Harper & Row, 1962), 2:398ff.; Frazier, *The Negro Church in America*, 47–81.

17. It is important to note that this thought is commensurate with that of the following scholars:

a. Gayraud Wilmore, who writes: "All of this is to say that the independent church movement among Blacks, during and immediately following the period of the Revolutionary War, must be considered, *ipso facto*, an expression of Black resistance to white oppression — *the first Black freedom movement.*" (*Black Religion and Black Radicalism*, 108).

b. John Hope Franklin, who writes: "Although Negroes took the initiative in bringing about separation, it appears that such steps were not taken until it was obvious that they were not welcome in the white churches. This keen sensitivity to mistreatment and the consequent organization of separate and independent religious organizations of their own were to be the cause for the church occupying such an important place in Negro life in the nineteenth and twentieth centuries." (*From Slavery to Freedom*, 164).

c. Eugene D. Genovese, who writes: "Then the black slaves of the New World made it their own, they transformed it into a religion of resistance — not often of revolutionary defiance, but of a spiritual resistance that accepted the limits of the politically possible. . . . Whereas the whites asked Jesus for forgiveness, the blacks primarily asked for recognition." (*Roll, Jordan, Roll: The World the Slaves Made* [New York: Pantheon Books, 1974], 254).

d. Harry V. Richardson, who writes: "Yet from the beginning the church served as the main outlet through which the slaves could express their sufferings and dissatisfaction. Although it was done covertly, the church rendered two great need services to the slaves: First, it kept alive the consciousness that the slave system was wicked; and second, it kept alive the hope that in the plan of a good, just God, the wicked, brutal system under which they lived would have to pass away." ("The Negro in American Religious Life," in *The American Negro Reference Book*, edited by John P. Davis [Englewood Cliffs, N.J.: Prentice-Hall, 1966], 401).

e. Lawrence Jones, who writes: "Black churches are also the product of the positive, self-affirming attitudes of Blacks toward themselves. They testify to the fact that Blacks had heard and believed the Gospel teaching that God is no respecter of persons. They were early aware of the distinction that had to be drawn between Christianity as practiced and preached by some whites and Christianity as proclaimed by its Founder." ("Black Churches in Historical Perspective," in *Christianity and Crisis 30*, no. 18 [November 12 and 16, 1970], 228).

f. See also a chapter devoted principally to this theme and its input for antebellum northern blacks in Monroe Fordham, *Major Themes in Northern Black Religious Thought, 1800–1860* (New York: Exposition Press, 1975), chap. 7.

18. Such threats are always present in the face of political movements, organizations, etc., that devalue the importance of religion or reject moral concerns while deliberating about methods for attaining desired goals. Similar threats attend those religious groups which devalue political involvements, i.e., those whose aims are primarily otherworldly. Both are alien to the black Christian tradition and fail to receive the legitimation of the community at large.

19. It is important to note that the Nation of Islam has characteristically explained itself to black Americans in terms of the black Christian tradition, explicating its symbols and sources while condemning the churches for their apostasy.

20. From the Quadrennial Address of the Bishops, *Journal of the 20th Quadrennial Session of the General Conference of the A.M.E. Church*, held in St. Stephens A.M.E. Church, Wilmington, N.C., May 4–22, 1896, 98.

21. Thus the concept of nonviolence as promulgated by Martin Luther King, Jr., was not alien to the black churches. None resisted it. In fact, King was merely explicating and implementing the traditional means of protest long practiced by the black churches under the black Christian tradition. King's novelty was in his method of mass demonstrations and bringing Gandhi's thought about nonviolent resistance into positive relationship with the black Christian tradition.

22. This has been one of the most disputed aspects of black theology which has been accused of bestowing ontological and ultimate significance on the concept blackness in contradistinction to that of whiteness.

23. The black Christian tradition represents an alternative position to

that of many neo-orthodox Protestant thinkers who draw radical distinctions between divine and human virtue.

24. It is worthy to note that more than a half century ago, H. Richard Niebuhr correctly perceived the cause of separation of black and white churches. "The dogma that divides the racial churches is anthropological, not theological, in content." See Niebuhr, *The Social Sources of Denominationalism*, 236.

25. Bishop R. R. Wright, *The Encyclopaedia of the African Methodist Episcopal Church*, 2nd ed. (Philadelphia: A.M.E. Publishing House, 1947), 625.

26. C. M. Tanner, *A Manual of the African Methodist Episcopal Church, Being a Course of Twelve Lectures for Probationers and Members* (Philadelphia: A.M.E. Publishing House, 1900), 104–6. It should also be noted that the above sentiment was expressed with similar clarity in the quadrennial address of the A.M.E. Church bishops in 1896 when they said: "Bishop Payne crystallized the sentiment of all the distinguished statesmen and churchmen when he said: 'God the Father; Christ our Redeemer; Man our Brother.' This is the official motto of the A.M.E. Church, and the mission in the commonwealth of Christianity is to bring all denominations and races to acknowledge and practice the sentiments contained therein. When these sentiments are universal in theory and practice, then the mission of the distinctive colored organizations will cease" (ibid., 98).

2

Autonomy in Dilemma

From the beginning of their history, white and black Americans have been in opposition to each other: whites constantly striving to dominate blacks, and blacks assiduously counteracting those efforts with various forms of resistance. This conflictual relationship has been rooted in two opposing views of humanity, the one contending that whites are genetically superior to blacks, and the other insisting that the races are inherently equal. The logic of each perspective has led to a corresponding set of values, attitudes, behavior patterns, theologies, social and political policies — in short, to two opposing worldviews. In other words, these respective perspectives have represented two fundamentally different philosophies of life which have designated the essential differences between the two races. Further, and most important for our purpose, the distinctive thought of the black churches has been grounded in its predominant view of humanity, which corresponds with what blacks perceive to be the basic biblical anthropology.

It is a curious fact, however, that black Americans have been intensely loyal to the basic goals and fundamental values of America in spite of the pervasive impact of racism. Ironically, their patriotism has been manifested in many ways, not the least of which is their zealous participation in all of the nation's wars as well as their full and uncritical support of the so-called American way of life. It should be quickly added, however, that black Americans have set themselves in opposition to white Americans on all issues pertaining to the problem of racism, while in everything else

27

that is typically American they have been prereflective, noncriti-
cal, and unambiguously supportive. This has led to a dilemma
with respect to racial self-understanding and national belonging,
a dilemma that W. E. B. DuBois called "double-consciousness."

> After the Egyptian and Indian, the Greek and Roman, the Teuton
> and Mongolian, the Negro is a sort of seventh son, born with a veil,
> and gifted with second-sight in this American world,—a world
> which yields him no true self-consciousness, but only lets him see
> himself through the revelation of the other world. It is a peculiar
> sensation, this double-consciousness, this sense of always looking at
> one's self through the eyes of others, of measuring one's soul by the
> tape of a world that looks on in amused contempt and pity. One ever
> feels his twoness—an American, a Negro; two souls, two thoughts,
> two unreconciled strivings; two warring ideals in one dark body,
> whose dogged strength alone keeps it from being torn asunder.
>   The history of the American Negro is the history of this strife,—
> this longing to attain self-conscious manhood, to merge his double
> self into a better and truer self. In this merging he wishes neither
> of the older selves to be lost. He would not Africanize America, for
> America has too much to teach the world and Africa. He would not
> bleach his Negro soul in a flood of white Americanism, for he knows
> that Negro blood has a message for the world. He simply wishes to
> make it possible for a man to be both a Negro and an American,
> without being cursed and spit upon by his fellows, without having
> the doors of Opportunity closed roughly in His face.
>   This, then, is the end of his striving; to be a co-worker in the king-
> dom of culture, to escape both death and isolation, to husband and
> use his best powers and his latent genius.[1]

We have quoted DuBois at length because his description of the
double-consciousness of black Americans is one of the clearest and
most accurate statements of black self-understanding in print. Its
truth has been echoed in countless other forms of racial self-
expression. Consequently, we find it a thoroughly helpful construct for explaining the moral and sociopolitical ambiguity that
appears so consistently in the history of the black churches. Its
importance cannot be overestimated, because it designates a
veritable contradiction at the heart of black existence. This cultural ambiguity has been demonstrated in two principal dilemmas
that are endemic to black American consciousness, namely, the

dilemmas of nation and religion. These represent, respectively, theories of politics and ecclesiology that imply moral conflicts in thought and practice. In other words, each of these theories gives rise to goals, rhetoric, and strategies which, upon careful analysis, reveal varying degrees of ambiguity. As we have indicated, this double-consciousness implies a double life with double thoughts, words, loyalties, ideals, practices, and the like. Even more devastating, DuBois concluded nearly a century ago: "From the double life every American Negro must live, as a Negro and as an American. . . . From this must arise a painful self-consciousness, an almost morbid sense of personality and a moral hesitancy which is fatal to self-confidence."[2] Let us look in greater depth at the nature of these respective dilemmas as they appear in the life and thought of the black churches.

THE NATIONAL DILEMMA

The national dilemma reveals itself in the dual loyalties that black Americans have to the nation, on the one hand, and to the race, on the other—conflicting loyalties because blacks have always felt a moral obligation to both the nation and the race in spite of the moral conflicts between them. Their loyalty to the nation emerged from the common plight of a race systematically forced to abandon most of its African culture and compelled to assimilate American values, attitudes, ideals, and customs. The loyalty of blacks to the race was forged by the ways in which they responded to their plight, responses that helped mold a common racial destiny in which they could take no small amount of pride. The main difference between the two loyalties was that the first was involuntary and the second was fully deliberate. The major moral problem this dilemma has presented to black Americans is that their respective loyalty to either race or nation implies a lack of loyalty to the other.

As the collective memory of the African past dwindled because of the impact of slavery on the familial, religious, and social structures of its victims, blacks found themselves born and reared in a subordinate and oppressed culture that had been shaped, in large part, by the dominant values of the nation at large. Those values, rooted in the prevailing ethos, aimed at making blacks feel that their associational life was a necessary aberration of the white paradigm. Thus the struggle of blacks for self-respect met headlong the predominant attitude of the larger society that believed unquestioningly in the incapacity of blacks for full human development. The collective resistance of the race to its oppressed condition resulted in the kind of solidarity that develops in any group that becomes aware of its common destiny. Ironically, the desired goal of black resistance to racism has always been full and equal participation in the life of the nation at large and in a way that would one day make the phenomenon of race both irrelevant and meaningless. That is to say, in the order of values in the black community loyalty to race has always been subordinate to the rights and privileges of full national citizenship. Thus the two conflicting loyalties are related to each other as oppressed condition is related to the dawn of liberation. In other words, the realization of the latter would necessarily render the values and experiences of the former insignificant. Had the Emancipation Act issued in full and equal citizenship for blacks, loyalty to race would have gradually disappeared, since its cohesive power would have been superseded by the uniting spirit of the national community. But the endurance of the dilemma has been due to the persistence of white racism and the institutionalization of black opposition to it.

Historically, the racial loyalty of blacks has constituted a major criterion for evaluating all policies emanating from white America. Blacks arrive at their moral judgments, in large part, by assessing the impact of specific policies, candidates, and programs on the race. Correspondingly, their loyalty to the nation has had an opposite effect. Rather than enabling the quest for racial justice, loyalty to the nation has often constituted a major constraint on the moral and political purposes of the race, because it has demanded a high measure of adaptation to the nation's major political and moral values. In fact, the loyalty of the black churches to the nation's laws and customs has often limited them in the kinds of action that they could advocate, especially when those laws and customs have been in conflict with the demands of racial justice. Strategies such as civil disobedience, armed struggle,

and various forms of underground activity have rarely been considered viable options by the black churches. Rather, it has been
customary for the black churches to demonstrate unceasingly, in
both thought and action, their strong patriotic spirit reified time
and again by their supreme sacrifices in the nation's many wars.

One of the perennial highlights of the conventions and the conferences of black Baptists and Methodists has been their respective
presidential and quadrennial addresses, all of which (among other
things) regularly editorialized on the state of the race as discerned
at the time. For many years, both the conventions and the conferences maintained standing committees charged with the task of
reporting regularly on "the state of the Negro in the nation,"
reports aimed at highlighting the major current issues of racial
injustice and advocating specific types of action, usually in the
form of letters of protest to the president of the United States and
occasionally to other governmental officials. A typical example of
such a report is seen in the record of the Twenty-fourth General
Conference of the African Methodist Episcopal (A.M.E.) Church,
which met in Kansas City in 1912. After setting forth two basic
propositions of faith, the committee proceeded to the heart of the
matter by carefully and graphically describing the nature of the
national dilemma. Both the form and the substance of this
description have a striking similarity to all of the reports, both
Baptist and Methodist, throughout the twentieth century.[3]

> First: we have abiding faith in the unshaken truth set forth in our
> denominational model, "God our Father, man our brother, Christ
> our Redeemer."
>
> Second: we have an abiding faith in the enlightening, converting
> and civilizing power of the gospel of Christ; and that this, through
> the help of God, makes the uplift, progress and development of
> mankind, irrespective of race, color, condition or country.
>
> We find, however, as it respects the loyal Negro citizen in the
> United States, that there are abundant facts evidencing that he is
> subjected to unjustifiable ostracisms, repressions, cruelties, disen-
> franchisements, lynchings, fraud, and misrepresentations in defi-
> ance of the tenets upon which our republic claims to the people of
> the world what it stands for, thus, by outrageous methods, nullify-
> ing the Constitutional Amendments and their guarantees as well as
> the protection that state laws claim to afford, thus depriving the

Negro citizen of his manhood rights. Yet, we observe encouraging counter forces operating on bringing the national mind to see the inconsistency of proclaiming this as the land of liberty to the oppressed, and at the same time permitting the oppressors to defy the plain declarations of our fundamental laws by refusing to protect the life, liberty, and happiness of ten millions of the country's most loyal and industrious citizens.[4]

Although the nature of the dilemma has been described similarly from one year to the next, the general assessment of the nation's disposition with respect to the dilemma has frequently changed. The 1912 report of the A.M.E. Church noted a small but important measure of improvement of the attitudes of whites toward blacks. "Negro opinion begins to be quoted and counted in national and municipal affairs. . . . This shows that men no longer disregard what the Negro may think on questions of public interest."[5] The report acknowledged approvingly that the opinions and actions of some whites with regard to racial justice provided grounds for hope.

> Answering to the growing integrity and power of this people, we see an increasing tendency to disprove the heresies of inborn inferiority, and to stand for equal opportunities and just enfranchisement of the Negro as a man and a citizen.
> The best thinkers of the other race are coming out in long delayed protest against lynching and prejudiced trials in order that they might protect the civilization and ideals of this republic. Thus, does God make it plain that the weal of one is the weal of all.[6]

In addition to the subtle optimism implied by measuring the progress of white attitudes toward the race question, this report, and many others like it, also took pains to measure the progress of the race in its march toward "civilization." Hitherto, black leaders had viewed the race as unready for the awesome task of assuming full social responsibility for themselves. As the years went by, however, black leaders developed a growing confidence in the race's capacity for self-determination, the evidence of which was its success in the development and expansion of black religious institutions. The leaders' hope was that this evidence would have a persuasive effect on whites and cause them to change their attitudes and their practices.

> There are two things necessary to the civilization and ennobling of any people:
> First: their inner growth and refinement.
> Second: the spirit of fair play among those with whom they live. The Negro is beyond all doubt improving in spiritual and psychical qualities: his education is becoming constantly broader, deeper and more useful in the practical affairs of life; his business interests are becoming larger and more closely entwined with the prosperity of the nation; his home life grows sweeter and more sacred day by day, and his race consciousness is merging into a realization that his manhood is a thing not dependent upon color or circumstances.[7]

Finally, the report changed its rhythm and content and charged the race to remain steadfast in the faith, self-respecting as a group, undaunted by the forces of racism, and confident of a high destiny in this nation.

> This General Conference, therefore, in the light of all these considerations declares to the world its pride and faith in its people; their history, their psychical power and their steady faith in their ultimate high destiny in this land of their birth.
> It declares that no degrading laws can smite our self-respect, or do more than reveal the bitterness and fear of the perpetrators. It declares that civilization can never go backward and that it cannot go forward without the dark race as well as the fair one.
> It declares that the retarding influences operating against us are accidental and transient, while those of growth and progress are natural, permanent and imbedded in the constitution of God's processes for bringing in His kingdom among men.
> It declares that it draws no race lines but acts in the face of those it finds strong, so as to protect its self-respect and manhood, until men become large enough to realize that we are all one in Jesus Christ; and here we shall ever stand, God being with us.[8]

Thus the typical structure of these reports on the state of the race in the nation reveals a fourfold pattern: (1) description of the dilemma, (2) assessment of the race's readiness for citizenship and its capacity to overcome the victimization of racial injustice, (3) assessment of the nation's capacity to do racial justice, and (4) confidence that God wills racial justice for human society and that its realization is possible in this nation.

Since the turn of the century the annual reports tended to depict a high measure of progress in the second category and a lesser degree in the third, while displaying virtually no change either in the description of the dilemma or in the black church leaders' confidence in the eschatological vision and its normative implications for human society. It should be said, however, that whenever a particular address or report failed to manifest the fourfold pattern, careful analysis of a series of similar reports or addresses by either the same or similar persons will show that this pattern was nevertheless functioning implicitly. Further, blacks have always believed that the Constitution of the United States explicitly embodies the norms of racial justice, and this belief has often served as the only empirical basis for their confidence in the nation's capacity for thinking and doing the right.[9] In his presidential address of 1898, Dr. E. C. Morris subtitled a section "The American Flag as Symbol." Here we see evidence of the first three sections of the fourfold pattern, with the fourth implied and later to be made explicit at the end of the entire address.

> That grand old flag is a significant symbol of every patriotic American. Its colors and peculiar arrangement are object lessons and inspire love for home and native land. To me it is an emblem of resplendent beauty. . . . Our race in this country, for many years held as slaves and not now enjoying the full complete protection of that flag, challenges the whole country to find a class of people more loyal. Whenever and wherever it has been placed in the hands of the ebony-hued sons of America its folds have not been allowed to trail in the dust. The American Negro can look through the "reign of terror" to which he has been subjected and from which he now suffers and see the ultimate triumph of those principles which lie at the very foundation of our government — that "all men are created equal and free," etc. He believed that the success of this flag in the Revolutionary War would bring a better day and followed it then; he followed it under Jackson without the hope of reward, and he saved it from dishonor in the Civil War; he also bravely led the charge under those colors at San Diego, and will ever remain loyal to it until this is indeed and in truth "the land of the free and the home of the brave."[10]

As already indicated, the fourth part of the fourfold pattern appeared at the end of Dr. Morris's address, providing the religious optimism characteristic of him and most of his predecessors and successors alike.

Do not think me pessimistic. I have faith in God and in the ultimate unity and triumph of our churches in this work, for I think I can see through the dim vista of time, as we go forward and grasp the problems of life and keep pace in the steady march of civilization, one Grand Army of Christian Believers; and I can hear the tramp of an unnumbered throng, like the voice of many waters, and, listening still I can hear the voice of that multitude as they raise the old battle cry of "One Lord, one faith, one baptism"; and in that grand procession, as they march against the powers of darkness, I can see the Galilean Jew sitting in the chariot with the Ethiopian eunuch, and their song is: "the kingdoms of this world are become the kingdoms of our Lord, and of his Christ; and he shall reign forever and ever."[11]

It must also be said that a loss of faith in the nation's capacity to do racial justice has always led to repudiation of the national dilemma, for such a disposition necessarily implies radical opposition to the nation per se and includes the conviction that the nation lacks the capacity to effect significant societal reform in race relations. Hence the logic of that position has led to the advocacy of one of three policies: (1) revolution, (2) colonization outside the nation, and (3) racial separation within the nation's borders. Although there is no evidence[12] that the churches ever officially took a revolutionary stance in relation to the nation, considerable discourse has focused from time to time on the idea of colonization both within and without the nation. In the main, however, it is important to note that any focus by the churches on either the development of Africa or the self-development of the race apart from whites has always been understood as a means to an end and never as an end in itself. In other words, the churches presumed that significant demonstration of the capacity for African and/or Afro-American self-development would convince white Americans that they should be granted full and complete citizenship rights. Thus, in that sense, the black churches have not been radical. They have rejected neither the basic religious nor the basic political orientation of the nation, while those who have done so have tended to depart from Christianity altogether or to convert to some other religion.

As we have said, the national dilemma has expressed itself in the perceptions that blacks have had concerning their dual loyalty to both nation and race. Considerable ambiguity has attended their affirmations of the nation as well as their valuations of the race itself and, more specifically, their assessment of the separate racial character of all black institutions, including their churches. On the one hand, they have affirmed the separation but, on the other, they have regretted it because of their commitment to the ideal of a fully integrated society wherein race has no positive social or political significance. Hence the high measure of racial pride felt in building, preserving, and expanding black institutions is dialectically related to their ideal of "one society." Similarly, blacks have agreed that the experience of separate religious development has been necessary in order to prove to themselves and to others that they are capable of "manhood Christianity" (a term coined in the nineteenth century to express the capacity of blacks for mature social leadership and to counter contrary views that they are childlike by nature and incapable of full human development).[13] Nevertheless, throughout the nineteenth century blacks felt no small amount of moral ambiguity in founding their separate churches. The choice between alternatives seemed always to be ominous: (1) compromising the principle of racial integration and (2) adapting to subordinate status within white churches.

This moral dilemma was fairly widespread during the early years following the founding of the National Baptist Convention. When President E. C. Morris delivered his annual presidential address in 1900, he sought to transcend this moral ambiguity by focusing on those who actually opposed the formation of a black Baptist denomination. He argued that blacks had no alternative but to demonstrate their capacities in separate racial development. Clearly his opposition was quelled somewhat by the events of the times: the Supreme Court decision, *Plessy* v. *Ferguson*, the rapid disfranchisement of blacks in the former Confederacy, and the ascendancy of racial segregation in all dimensions of black existence.

> We have endeavoured to exercise great patience and charity toward those who seemed to think a National Convention of Negro Baptists unnecessary, as we are sure that time and environment will be sufficient to convince them of the necessity of such an organization. To

me, as the "heavens declare the glory of God," so do the signs of the times in church and in State point to the fact that for the Negro to ever be received and given the place of a man in religion, in politics, in business, etc., he must accumulate, he must own, control, or manage enterprises for the development of the race and the blessing of mankind. . . .

The conditions in this country have forced the Negroes to be separate in their churches, associations, and conventions, from their white brethren, and these smaller organizations have, by reason of the same conditions, been forced to form this national convention.[14]

Elsewhere in the same address Morris stated quite unambiguously that the purpose of the convention was to enable "the complete development of the Negro as a man along all lines, beginning first with his religious life, and ending with the material, or business life."[15]

The dilemma of loyalty to nation and to race is clearly revealed in the latter part of Morris's address, which we quote at length for two reasons: (1) it depicts the logic of alternative views and why they were not acceptable to the majority of blacks, and (2) it contains the typical arguments that have been set forth year after year by the leaders of the convention in support of black churches.

Our race and people in America are, like the unwary waters of the mighty deep, impatient, irrepressible, and determined upon the amelioration of their condition. We do not condemn this spirit of anxiety in them, but, we should bear in mind that only twenty-five years have passed since the march to a state of cultivated citizenship and high Christian motive was begun. We all deprecate the fact that conditions have arisen to darken the future of the black man in this country. We all regret that racial conflicts have taken place in any part of this glorious land, and that the spirit to disregard the laws of the country has grown in the last decade to marvellous proportions. But this disregard for the law does not represent the best element of our citizens or the true spirit of Americanism. Crime should and must be punished — but there is no doubt as to the fact that the utter disregard for law and order has produced a feeling of unrest all over the country, which has presented a serious problem to both the white and black races in the United States. This problem, however, is being considered in the counsel of both races by their wisest and best men, and it is my firm conviction that it will meet with satisfactory solution before another generation is passed. Many of our good and great men have suggested as a means to the solution of the problem rising out of the race conflicts such theories as African emigration, the industrial training of the Negro masses, colonization, etc. But it appears that none of the plans proposed meets the approval of a very large number of our people. The majority of the Negroes believe themselves to be American citizens by every right to which any can lay claim, and cherish the hope that pluck, energy, economy, and accumulation along material lines will eventually solve the problem. Racial prejudice cannot be removed in a single generation, except in those cases where the religious nature dominates all others, and this, as you know, is a rare thing. What the black man cannot understand is that for the first ten years after his emancipation when he was least prepared for the enjoyment of his civil and political rights he received these rights and the encouragement and apparent good will of all. But after having come in contact with the schoolhouse and the church, and begun to be more and more a man, there sprang up a unanimous action in the South to deprive him of those rights. There cannot be the slightest doubt that many of the persons today who were born in slavery have improved every opportunity since their emancipation, to show themselves as men, and *nothing can come now to make them believe themselves less than men.*

But having these things to face, is it not well to consider whether or not they are blessings in disguise? Do they not more and more tend to throw the race on its own responsibilities, and thereby establish the fact that it can be a race of resources? My brethren, these things mean to me that the Negroes are to be owners of farms, dry goods stores, groceries; that we are to have grain dealers, cotton factories, and, in short, are to be actually associated with the business interests of the world. . . . When we take into account the outside agencies which God has at work in our behalf, coupled with the unprecedented efforts being put forth by the race and denomination, we will enter the twentieth century under conditions which to me are most encouraging.

We should bear with patience all the indignities heaped upon us, by those who have apparently lost all respect for the fundamental laws of our great country. And yet, we should contend with manly courage, in a Christian way, for every right enjoyed by any other people under the flag of our nation.[16]

The complexity of the above argument is perhaps not immediately self-evident. But when one considers that such different black leaders as W. E. B. DuBois and Booker T. Washington[17] (whose historic debate[18] constituted a long and bitter struggle) could both agree with virtually everything Morris said, one is made aware of the ambiguous character of Morris's argument. Morris's focus on civil rights revealed his affirmation of ideas that were also the salient characteristics of DuBois' thought, namely, confidence in "the talented tenth" of both races as being racially just, the disregard for law and order on the part of white racists, and the absolute commitment of blacks to improve their condition and insist on being treated with dignity. Similarly, his beliefs that racial prejudice could not be eradicated in a single generation, that racial discrimination was "a blessing in disguise" because it forced blacks to develop their own resources, that the burden of racial injustice should be borne with patience, that blacks should work eagerly within the law for every right enjoyed by others, revealed the basic principles of Booker T. Washington's philosophy.

Thus Morris's speech contained elements that have often led to divergent social policies when advocated apart from one another. Most religious leaders of major black institutions, including Morris, have personified this dilemma in their thought and action, notwithstanding the official statements of their respective institutions. In the light of this we conclude that the Washington-DuBois debate dramatized the two horns of this dilemma. Neither disagreed in principle with the other's position, but both advocated different strategies and priorities in the deployment of resources and energies.

Black religious leaders saw more clearly than either Washington or DuBois that the roots of their respective positions lay in the traditions of the black churches, since the latter had wrestled with the same dilemma from the beginning of their history: (1) the desire for first-class citizenship rights in a racially integrated society, and (2) separate racial development in the religious, social, and economic dimensions of their life as a necessary condition for political rights. Thus it was not difficult for the black Baptist and the Methodist denominations to welcome both DuBois and Washington regularly to their assemblies, although it was politic not to have them on the same platform at the same time. Their basic perspectives and strategies had long been legitimated and practiced by the churches. The churches' embrace of DuBois was commensurate with their indentification with the abolition movement, Reconstructionism, and the subsequent mission of such organizations as the National Association for the Advancement of Colored People (NAACP) and the Southern Christian Leadership Conference (SCLC). Similarly, their strong affirmation of Booker T. Washington was in accord with their tradition of racial self-development in the formation of independent black churches, fraternal societies, and businesses, all of which provided the basis for their socioeconomic development. Their later support of such organizations as the National Urban League, the National Negro Business League, and People United to Save Humanity evidences the continuation of that tradition up to the present day. Clearly, for the most part the churches at the national level had the capacity to contain the dilemma and all of its ambiguity both in sentiment and in practice.[19] In that respect, the churches have served the race as an important cohesive force.

During the nascent period of their institutional development, blacks were quite self-conscious about the dilemma caused by their loyalty to a racially separate church and their faithfulness to the ideal of an integrated society. But by the late nineteenth century, the matter hardly ever was raised by either the African Methodist Episcopal Church or the African Methodist Episcopal Zion Church because of their growing pride in a century of progress and the "taken-for-grantedness" of such ventures. As with the Baptists, however, it was certainly present in the beginning of African Methodism. In his so-called Declaration of Independence, Richard Allen said the following in the preamble: "Whereas, from time to time many inconveniences have arisen from white people and people of color mixing together in public assemblies, more particularly places of worship, we have thought it necessary to provide for ourselves a convenient house to assemble in, separate from the white brethren."[20] Obviously the separation was viewed as a necessity rather than an ideal. The Declaration went on to state three reasons for the separation: (1) to prevent whites from being offended by the presence of blacks at worship; (2) to prevent blacks from getting a distorted view of Christianity and especially its understanding of the nature of humanity; and (3) to help uplift the race from the degradation of its slave past. While the first reason led some to condemn Allen's independence church movement as a sign of black submission to racial segregation, the second provided both religious and political justification for the church's history of protest against racial injustice. The third reason constituted the foundation for racial self-development and its concomitant virtues of racial self-respect, good moral character, thrift, obedience to the law, and independence of spirit. All of these virtues were personified by Allen himself and institutionalized in the thought and practice of the African Methodist Episcopal Church.

Once again we can see clearly that if any one of the above reasons were to be isolated from the others and made the basis for one's thought and action, the result could lead to quite different orientations to the world on the part of both individuals and groups. While that has happened from time to time in various parts of the African Methodist Episcopal Church, as well as in other churches, African Methodism nevertheless has had a peculiar genius for unifying this variety in such a way there has not as yet been an institutional split over these matters. The function of the episcopacy in preserving order and unity may have been a major reason for this.

THE ECCLESIASTICAL DILEMMA

Just as Martin Luther, John Wesley, and others had no desire to form new churches, so also the founders of the black church independence movement would have chosen otherwise had viable options been available to them. Some evidence of the desire of white churches for racial justice would have constituted the grounds for such an alternative. But, to the contrary, the white churches reflected in their thought and practice the same patterns of interracial relationships that characterized the society as a whole. In fact, the churches readily provided religious justification for racial inequality, thus sanctifying the society's laws and customs concerning it. Hence this collaboration of church and society made it difficult for white Americans to perceive any immorality in their interracial relationships. In comparison with the perceptions of blacks, one discovers two distinctly different worlds of existence and meaning.

It did not take blacks long to perceive the social implications of the biblical view of humanity or the nature of their unjust condition when considered in relation to the guiding principles of the American Revolution, self-evident truths of the Constitution, the American concept of religious liberty, and their own innate sense of fairness. For these and other reasons, the white slave masters understandably viewed Christianity as a dangerous tool in the hands of blacks. Consequently they deliberated for many decades before promoting the conversion of blacks to Christianity and, later, granting them the opportunity to worship by themselves. That the slave masters were always uncomfortably aware of the implicit dangers of rebellion inherent in both the Christian religion and the nation's constitution has been pointed out repeatedly by Gayraud Wilmore and others: "The possibility of slave uprisings was invariably associated with Black religion, despite the pains that had been taken to make Christianity an instrument of compliancy and control. Black Christians who were ardent about their religion had to be watched carefully."[21]

For obvious reasons the fears were not so great when the black churches were controlled by whites, but the birth of black independent churches heightened the anxiety level considerably. The irony of the situation is seen in the fact that whites did not want to worship with blacks on an equal basis, nor were whites eager to allow blacks to worship by themselves. Rather, they preferred to have blacks worship with them in a subordinate status. Not surprisingly, all black religious leaders had immense difficulties trying to effect institutional separation from their white brethren, to say nothing of the many exasperating problems they had in their efforts to ensure continuity in the episcopal orders.[22]

Just as the persistent resistance of blacks to racial oppression and their survival as a race prove that the sway of racism in America has never been absolute, so also the ecclesiastical separation of blacks from whites has never been absolute. Rather, varying forms of informal and contractual alliances[23] and common inherited traditions in polity, discipline, theology, hymnody, professional training, vestments, rituals, and the like, have endured, with little attempt to alter their substance in any significant way.[24] This does not deny important stylistic and emotive changes in these traditions by way of music and song, style of preaching, and other aesthetic forms. More important, the main substantive contribution the black churches have made to Christian belief and practice is the fundamental commitment to the anthropological principle of the equality of all persons under God. This has constituted the essence of black Christianity in America and has found expression in many novel forms of music, song, liturgy, preaching, and styles of leadership. In their churches, blacks could escape from racial suppression and subordination and affirm a view of humanity different from that promulgated by white churches. In this respect, there is no difference between black Methodists and black Baptists. Rather, they have more in common than either has with its own white counterpart.

In relation to internal decision-making processes, the black churches in the main have been independent of the white churches. At the same time, they have chosen to remain in continuity with these traditions from which they separated. This has constituted an ecclesiastical dilemma involving no small amount of moral and political ambiguity. The act of disassociation through institutional separation has been dialectically related to the strong desires of the black churches to remain in some looser form of association with their white counterparts and, to this end, associational relationships have been contractually forged regularly by the respective bodies. Needless to say, the mission of the black churches has been peculiarly affected by this situation.

A major surprise for the student of the black church independence movement is the discovery that white clergy were employed to pastor black congregations of the African Methodist Episcopal Zion Church during the first two decades of its existence.[25] Even more surprising is the fact that at the first conference of the African Methodist Episcopal Zion Church, the Reverend William Phoebus of the Methodist Episcopal Church presided in order to ensure apostolic legitimacy — since no blacks had been ordained at that time. As long as the dispositions of the respective white ministers were friendly and seemingly free of racial prejudice, the black churches had no difficulty in principle with their leadership function. Similarly, the black Baptist conventions have always been in various forms of association with their white counterparts, the most enduring relationship being the joint sponsorship of the American Baptist College of the American Baptist Theological Seminary, jointly owned and controlled since the 1920s by the Southern Baptist Convention and the National Baptist Convention, U.S.A., Inc. These and other cooperative endeavors manifested a total lack of racial hostility on the part of the black church independence movement and clearly demonstrated that the latter was a reform movement rather than a revolutionary one. The many attempts of the African Methodist Episcopal Zion Church to reunite with the Methodist Episcopal Church on the full basis of equality also evidences its desired goal and implicit trust.[26]

As with the nation, black churches have made most of the prominent causes of the white churches their causes, such as prohibition, temperance, sexual laxity, gambling, smoking, dancing, divorce, revivalism, and foreign missions. Although their commitment to these issues aided the task of constructing a viable social order in the black community patterned after the social norms promulgated by the white churches, these issues have often appeared to take precedence over the original purposes of the black church independence movement which aimed at religious, moral, and political freedom from racial oppression. The moral dilemma is seen in their understanding of Christian moral formation, namely, the development of law-abiding, respectable citizens whose diligence in work, thrift in consumption, gentle manners, good character, and patient spirit contributed to the maintenance of peace and harmony between the races. In our judgment, as long as the churches thought and acted in that way they constituted no actual threat to the oppressive structures of the larger society but in a sense contributed unwittingly to the maintenance of the status quo. In their drive to prove that they were capable of "manhood Christianity" and responsible citizenship, they expended enormous

amounts of energy on the internal affairs of institutional development. Since the churches viewed this as a means to the desired goal
of being treated justly by whites, they perceived no problem with
such an orientation. For several generations they had placed their
confidence in the belief that the problem was basically one of
ignorance on the part of whites. Consequently they believed that
after whites became enlightened with empirical evidence they in
turn would forthrightly alter their racial attitudes and practices.
But herein lies another problem. The black churches' tendency to
promote a "soft" nationalism (i.e., a temporary experiment in
racial self-development) dissipated all inclinations toward working
for long-term goals of consolidated economic and political power.
This is not intended to imply that the churches had no long-term
goals or that they intentionally decided against such objectives.
But since such goals would have necessitated a different ideal
societal vision, the black churches gave very little attention to
them. In short, their ideal vision of a racially integrated society
militated against most long-term strategies necessary for the race's
full development. Thus, ironically, the long years of commitment
to "racial uplift" on the part of the black churches were destined
to nonfulfillment, because their ideal vision contradicted the idea
of separate racial development. The official needs of the black
denominations are replete with evidence showing that the thought
and action of the black churches have been guided more by their
ideal vision of a racially integrated society than by the idea of
racial development.

Moreover, this ideal vision led many blacks to measure their
achievements and priorities according to the predominant norms
of the white society, and this contributed to a peculiar type of psychological formation whereby blacks have often tended to view
their own accomplishments as necessarily inferior to those of
whites. Concomitantly, blacks have often exhibited a tendency to
develop certain compensatory needs evidenced in the desire for the
approval of whites in all that they do. Thus the inclusion of a white
person or of white persons, official or otherwise, on special programs (opening sessions of conferences and conventions, funerals,

memorial services, groundbreaking ceremonies, and the like) has always had its own peculiar import for both the psyches of individuals and the spirit of the group.

It is also ironic that, regardless of motive, the cooperation of the white churches was often an indispensable condition for the emergence and development of black independent churches. The following reasons are significant: (1) The founders of the black churches had no intention of founding churches that were distinct from their white counterparts on matters of policy and doctrine, and hence took considerable care to ensure a continuing positive relationship with them;[27] (2) the condition of the freemen in the northern cities during the antebellum period (i.e., the early period of African Methodism) and the increasing disfranchisement of blacks throughout the South during the decade following the end of Reconstruction (i.e., the early years of the National Baptist Convention) made it necessary for black church leaders to have some white friends in order to acquire property, bank loans, mortgages, and the like;[28] and (3) the general lack of economic resources and trained clergy rendered black churches vulnerable to the encouragement of benevolent assistance from white churches and various philanthropic agencies.

But the most important reason for desiring a continuing association with the white churches lay in the moral and social implications of that ideal societal vision that has always inspired the black churches, namely, the vision of a society in which race would have no significance. Consequently any positive form of association, regardless of the implicit paternalism that inevitably characterized it, symbolized the partial realization of their ultimate desire. It mattered not that the association was imperfect; what mattered most was that a small measure of racial justice was experienced through these cooperative associations. And that provided an experiential basis for the hope that their vision of society would one day be fulfilled.[29]

The national and international conferences and conventions of the Methodist and Baptist churches have afforded the black denominations considerable opportunity for interracial relationships. Blacks have been prominently represented in the world con-

ferences of their respective denominations since the late nineteenth
century and frequently as leading speakers and participants. They
have also been zealous supporters of the ecumenical movement
and were represented at the 1910 conference in Edinburgh that led
to the eventual formation of the World Council of Churches. At
the WCC's first meeting in Amsterdam, Bishop W. J. Walls took
the initiative in causing the Council to place representatives from
the black denominations on the Central Committee.

> When the nominating committee made its first report, Bishop
> W. J. Walls, delegate representing the A.M.E. Zion Church,
> obtained the platform and stated that there were member churches
> of this body containing memberships of about 15 million people in
> America who had no representative on the Central Committee and
> made the motion that representation should be placed on the com-
> mittee. The presiding officer, the Archbishop of Canterbury, put the
> motion immediately, and it carried. The Assembly thus approved
> the Central Committee which included the first two black Ameri-
> cans, Dr. Benjamin E. Mays, representing the National Baptists and
> Bishop W. J. Walls representing the three black Methodist denomi-
> nations.
>
> These two men served for six years. . . . After the Second Assem-
> bly held in Evanston, Illinois in 1954, they were succeeded by Dr.
> Joseph H. Jackson (Baptist) and Bishop D. Ward Nichols (A.M.E.).[30]

Thus even in the international assemblies black Americans have
had to be on their guard against the possibility of exclusion. Usually, however, they have experienced a greater spirit of acceptance
in international gatherings than at home. Their full participation
in many similar associations, including the various world Sunday
school movements, international and national Christian Endeav-
our, and Christian education organizations, has brought vicarious
satisfaction to millions of their constituents.

It is significant also that the black denominations were present
at the 1905 Inter-Church Conference on Federation which led to
the formation of the Federal Council of Churches. Bishop Alexander Walters of the A.M.E. Zion Church served on its executive
committee. In 1950 Bishops William J. Walls (A.M.E. Zion) and
Sherman L. Greene (A.M.E.) led the procession of signers of the
charter that established the National Council of the Churches of

Christ in the U.S.A. The A.M.E. Zion Church led the black denominations with their contribution of $10,000 to the Inter-church Center at 475 Riverside Drive, New York, for a memorial conference room in honor of two of their distinguished bishops: James Varick, founder and first bishop of their church, and W. J. Walls, a recognized leader in the ecumenical movement.[31]

Despite their devotion and loyalty to the ecumenical movement nationally and internationally, the spirit of independence that had always motivated the black denominations and inspired their mission assumed a black ecumenical expression in 1934 with the formation of the National Fraternal Council of Churches.

> The organization began as the Negro Fraternal Council of Churches at Chicago, in 1934. It later comprised 12 black denominations, representing 7,000,000 members; A.M.E., A.M.E. Zion and C.M.E., the Central Jurisdiction of the Methodist Church, the two leading National Baptist Conventions, the African Orthodox Church, the Freewill Baptist, the Church of God in Christ, the Apostolic Churches, the Bible Way Church of Washington, D.C., Church of God and Saints of Christ, and the Metropolitan Community Church of Chicago (twelve denominations).
>
> The purposes of the organization were: (1) To develop cooperative relations among all member denominations, and to take appropriate collective measures to strengthen this bond of Christian Unity, so that they may work together as one United Church to bring about racial and economic justice, progressive measures of non-partisan political legislation and social reform. (2) To afford a center for coordinating the actions of the denominations in the achievement of their common goals. (3) To cooperate with other organizations of like nature in seeking to foster the world-wide program of Christ.[32]

The formation of the National Fraternal Council of Churches evidenced an inevitable pattern in race relations in America. Whenever blacks are members of predominantly white institutions and associations, they seem unable to rise to a place of preeminence, that is, to a place of leadership with power and authority. Further, the basic concerns of blacks seem never to be given high priority in those places. Bishop Walls said of this new black council of churches:

The National Fraternal Council of Churches was an assertion of the black religious leader on the same platform of Christian unity as other ecumenical movements. It gave him opportunity to express himself on vital issues, especially those appertaining to the rights of black people of America and their deepest concerns. . . . It was a vigilante group on all the issues that pertained to the well-being, the freedom, the religious and political equality, and the outstanding fight for a balanced and progressive social activism in the nation's whole life, especially in education, religion and civil rights.[33]

The viability of the organization continued for three decades, diminishing in the mid-1960s. Several attempts have been made in the 1970s to revive the spirit of the organization in a new form.

Not only has the ecclesiastical dilemma manifested itself in the conflict of the black churches over their dual loyalties to independent institutional development, on the one hand, and the maintenance of associational relationships with white churches, on the other, but it has also revealed itself in the ambiguous sentiments that black religious leaders have long held concerning themselves. Most black religious nationalists, like most black political nationalists, were at one time in their lives strong advocates of the ideal vision of a racially integrated society. When their hopes for its realization had died, they converted to the "radical left wing." Although the total number of such conversions has been small, it nevertheless has comprised such significant persons as Henry Highland Garnett (Presbyterian), Daniel Coker (A.M.E.), Bishop Henry McNeil Turner (A.M.E.), Bishop Theodore Holly (Episcopal), Bishop Lucius H. Holsey (C.M.E.), Alexander Crummell (Episcopal), Edward Wilmot Blyden (Presbyterian), Moses Dickson (A.M.E.), Charles Satchell Morris (Baptist), and Lewis G. Jordan (Baptist), to mention only a few who have been immortalized in the annals of black American religion. It should be noticed that several of those named above were not members of black denominations, and that should dispel any presuppositions that black churches and leaders in predominantly white denominations are less likely to become left-wing religious radicals. Possibly the reverse is more likely. In any case, denominational affiliation does not appear to be a significant variable in this regard.

In his argument against the opinion that black religion was basically a conservative, otherworldly type of phenomenon, Gayraud Wilmore shows how black religion has nurtured and produced insurrectionists, emigrationists, domestic separatists, and even a few revolutionaries. Wilmore also shows how those persons and institutions thought to be "harmless" frequently have many surprising ambivalences and ambiguities. He argues further that the restraint that the black ministers employed during slavery not to lead uprisings "had nothing to do either with the otherworldliness of their faith, or the cowardice of their personal lives."[34] He goes on to argue that the same kind of restraint is utilized week after week throughout the universe of black religious leadership. Although the black churches have a long history of opposition to violence, they have frequently vascillated between violence and nonviolence, especially during periods of intense racial hostility. And even when they were not prepared to advocate violence per se, their reasons were usually practical ones, namely, that it would be ineffective for such a minority to confront the power of America's military might. Nevertheless, the veiled threat of a racial bloodbath has often been implied by the most patriotic of black leaders.

After twenty-seven consecutive years of presidential leadership in the National Baptist Convention, Dr. E. C. Morris's final annual address was read posthumously. Many referred to him as a "conservative," and he chose in that address to describe the sense in which he was such.

> It would be needless repetition to recount the marvellous activities of the race since we were emancipated. But what do these achievements amount to if we are not to be counted free American citizens? I think you know that I have stood for absolute equality of the races under the laws of our country, believing the time would come when the color of a man's skin would be no bar to his rights as an American citizen. Upon these questions I have been glad to be counted conservative.[35]

He went on to say that he had never viewed all whites as enemies of the race, for many were true friends. But he admitted that even these had been powerless to effect racial justice. He ques-

tioned the worthiness of those white leaders who talk about racial
justice but seem unable to bring lynchers before the courts.

> It cannot be that our white friends think that we shall ever be satis-
> fied with anything less than absolute equality before the law for
> while there is one Negro left, he will contend for justice and equal-
> ity from the powers that be.[36]

This remark entailed more courage than will immediately
appear evident to the contemporary reader, because it called not
only for justice but for equality, the latter being virtually
anathema in most sections of the country at that time. Nevertheless Morris claimed that racial justice was a necessary condition if
blacks were to remain Christians, implying that should they leave
the Christian faith, their commitment to the virtues of love, peace,
and goodwill would cease. Herein is the veiled threat already
alluded to previously.

> I may be criticized for devoting this much of my address to racial
> matters, but my only apology is that, unless we can in what may be
> termed a Christian land, secure for our race, from the dominant
> race such privileges to which they are entitled, we cannot hope to
> hold them in the Christian religion. It is evident that if Christ is
> unable with the millions of white and colored Christians in America
> to bring about better conditions for his Negro followers, he is unable
> to redeem a single soul and unworthy to be followed. . . . We early
> imbibed the religion of the white man; we believed in it; we believe
> in it now, and hope never to be divorced from it; but if that religion
> does not mean what it says, if God did not make of one blood all
> nations of men to dwell on the face of the earth, and if we are not
> to be counted as part of that generation, by those who handed the
> oracle down to us, the sooner we abandon them or it, the sooner we
> will find our place in a religious sect in the world. It is not enough
> to have our white friends express goodwill, and offer and give us
> help. If the American ideal — viz. freedom of thought, freedom of
> speech, the right to property and to be protected in every right guar-
> anteed under the Constitution of the United States — is not given us,
> then we should in mass rise up and leave our churches, and schools,
> and our homes as a rendezvous for reptiles, owls, bats, and every
> hateful bird and seek asylum among a people who will recognize
> merit in any man regardless of his color, creed or condition. Are
> there such countries? Assuredly there are, and our people should be
> made acquainted with them.[37]

Even though Morris went on to say that blacks in general, and he in particular, harbored no hatred in their hearts for whites, one can readily see how easily a shift in circumstance could lead to a shift in logic and a completely reversed orientation to the nation, its laws, customs, and religion. In other words, the black churches and their leaders have always been in a state of readiness, at least theoretically, to move from a so-called conservative mode into quite a different style, depending upon the circumstances. Nowhere is that reality seen more clearly than in such statements as that contained in the *Christian Recorder* in 1890 when a quarterly conference of the African Methodist Episcopal Church in Virginia took place at the same time as two black men—believed by all to be innocent—were hanged. Rev. Robert Davis wrote:

> Our people were at a loss what to do. Some said the quarterly meeting would not go on and then came to me to know about it. I told them yes, the meeting would go on just the same. I told them that the white people had been hanging our people for nearly three hundred years and it was not worth while for me to stop my meeting. So we went on and had more people present than ever before. We prayed, we sang and preached as though no one had been hanged, notwithstanding the occasion was one of great solemnity—an awful time. These men faced death boldly and in a firm voice protested their innocence, and said, "it was hard to die for an infamous offense of which they were not guilty." How long, oh Lord, with greatest depths will colored men have to stand on the scaffolds of the South and plead for their innocence in vain? O, Lord, that thy judgments may sit on our oppressors. Our people generally believe that these parties were innocent, hence it has inspired deep unrest and dissatisfaction among the colored people here.[38]

It should not take much imagination to perceive in such a statement the ambivalent sentiments of the author and the implied restraint exercised both by him and by those whom he represented. The history of the black churches has been replete with similar circumstances and similar responses.

NOTES

1. W. E. B. DuBois, *The Souls of Black Folk*, in *Three Negro Classics* (New York: Avon Books, 1965), 214-15.

2. Ibid., 346.

3. See the presidential addresses delivered annually at the National Baptist conventions and the quadrennial addresses of the bishops delivered regularly at the national conferences of the African Methodist Episcopal Churches, as well as the reports of any special committees on the state of the race in the nation.

4. "Report of the Committee on the condition of the Negro in the United States to the 24th General Conference of the A.M.E. Church, Kansas City, Mo., May 20, 1912," in John Thomas Jenifer, *Centennial Retrospect: History of the A.M.E. Church* (Nashville: Sunday School Union Print, 1915), 311.

5. Ibid., 316.

6. Ibid.

7. Ibid., 311–12.

8. Ibid., 316.

9. Nowhere is this made clearer than in a statement made by Dr. J. H. Jackson, president of the National Baptist Convention U.S.A., Inc., under the title "Reaffirmation of Our Faith in the Nation," which also exhibits the fourfold pattern. See *The Record of the 79th Annual Session of the National Baptist Convention, U.S.A., Inc., held with the Baptist churches of San Francisco, California, September 9–13, 1959* (Nashville: Sunday School Publishing Board, 1959), 258–59. It has also been reprinted as Appendix B in Peter J. Paris, *Black Leaders in Conflict* (New York: Pilgrim Press, 1978), 232–33.

10. E. C. Morris, *Sermons, Addresses and Reminiscences and Important Correspondence with a Picture Gallery of Eminent Ministers and Scholars* (Nashville: National Baptist Publishing Board, 1901), 80–81.

11. Ibid., 86–87.

12. Although there is no evidence of official involvement, the A.M.E. Church was indirectly implicated in the Denmark Vesey rebellion of 1822 through Vesey himself, who had been a lay preacher in the A.M.E. Church, and Morris Brown, who allegedly served as a secret counselor to the plotters who planned their activity in an A.M.E. Church. (See Carol V. R. George, *Segregated Sabbaths: Richard Allen and the Emergence of Independent Black Churches, 1760–1840* (New York: Oxford University Press, 1973), 109–110.

13. We should avoid the temptation to read into the term "manhood Christianity" merely the judgments gained from the thought of present-day feminists. Male chauvinism, per se, was not the aim in spite of the sexism of the day that is expressed by the term. In short, we should not lose sight of the main issue seeking expression in spite of the sexist language.

14. *Journal of the Twentieth Annual Session of the National Baptist Convention held in the Fifth Street Baptist Church, Richmond, Virginia,*

September 12–17, 1900 (Nashville: National Baptist Publishing Board, 1900), 24–25.

15. Ibid., 29.

16. Ibid., 34–35.

17. Both DuBois and Washington made several annual appearances at the National Baptist convention for the purpose of delivering significant addresses. They also appeared at the General Conference of the A.M.E. Church.

18. The basic arguments of each side are clearly set forth in the following: "Of Mr. Booker T. Washington and Others," in W. E. B. DuBois, *The Souls of Black Folk*, 240ff.; Booker T. Washington's Atlanta Exposition Address in his autobiography, *Up from Slavery*, in *Three Negro Classics* (New York: Avon Books, 1965), 146ff.

19. But the National Baptist Convention, U.S.A., Inc., for example, was not always able to contain that dilemma. In 1961 the convention was split under the leadership of Martin Luther King, Jr., and some of his strongest supporters largely over the issue of the Convention's position on the strategy of nonviolent resistance, which became muddled with a number of other issues. The result of the split was the formation of the Progressive National Baptist Convention. None of the black Methodist churches have had splits.

20. Charles H. Wesley, *Richard Allen, Apostle of Freedom* (Washington, D.C.: Associated Publishers, 1935), 79–80.

21. Gayraud Wilmore, *Black Religion and Black Radicalism* (New York: Doubleday & Co., 1972), 104.

22. A typical example of this difficulty is detailed by Carol V. R. George. It depicts the struggles Richard Allen had with the Methodist Episcopal Church to effect complete independence — a struggle that was finally resolved by a court judgment (George, *Segregated Sabboths*, 49ff.). Similar difficulties attended the struggle of the A.M.E. Zion Church in its effort to gain independence. See William J. Walls, *The African Methodist Episcopal Zion Church: Reality of the Black Church* (Charlotte, N.C.: A.M.E. Zion Church Publishing House, 1974), 77ff.

23. Bishop Richard Allen's *Book of Discipline* set forth a strong anti-slavery statement and a clause that limited officeholding to Africans. But everything else was taken virtually verbatim from the discipline of the parent group. Further, the fact that Bishop Francis Asbury dedicated the mother church of the African Methodist Episcopal Church and named it "Bethel" is not an isolated event but, rather, an indication that on frequent occasions black independent churches even sought the official recognition of the white denominations from which they had departed.

24. It is important to note that while reflecting on the purpose of Richard Allen, Bishop C. M. Tanner reminds us that Allen decided to hold to the doctrines, beliefs, and form of government as taught by Wesley and

practiced by Methodists. "Allen was no advocate of church divisions; he had read with trembling, the thundering imprecations against all who dare to rend the visible body of the Savior; hence, when compelled to leave, let it be said to his praise, that he made no attempt to bring in a new ministry, or to institute rites and ceremonies not authorized by the Church" (C. M. Tanner, *A Manual of the African Methodist Episcopal Church, Being a Course of Twelve Lectures for Probationers and Members* [Philadelphia: A.M.E. Publishing House, 1900], 19). It is also significant to note Tanner's statement about the lack of dispute concerning doctrine in the A.M.E. Church. "Hence, while other religious bodies have been torn and rent, yes, even their very existence itself threatened by disputes about doctrine, our church has been singularly free from all such strife. Heresy trials are almost unknown among us" (ibid., 101–102). Similarly, the black Baptists accepted fully the basic historical principles of Baptists, namely, believer's baptism; belief in Jesus Christ as Lord and Savior as the only necessary statement of belief; the autonomy of the local church; the Scriptures as the sole authority on all matters of faith and practice. In this respect, there appears to be no difference between black and white Baptists. But, implicitly, the difference is virtually the same as that of black Methodists.

25. James T. Haley, *Afro-American Encyclopaedia; or, The Thoughts, Doings and Sayings of the Race* (Nashville: Haley and Florida, 1896), 443.

26. David Henry Bradley, Jr., *A History of the A.M.E. Zion Church, Vol. 2, 1872–1968* (Nashville: Parthenon Press, 1970), 319ff.

27. As we have pointed out, Richard Allen accepted fully all of the doctrines of the Methodist Church and thus gave no grounds for being called a schismatic (Tanner, *Manual*, 101ff.). Similarly, Richard Allen was ordained by Bishop Francis Asbury in order to demonstrate the apostolic continuity of the African Methodist Episcopal Church with worldwide Methodism. Also, black Baptists have neither rejected nor modified any of the cardinal principles of Baptists.

28. From 1895 onward the Southern Baptist Convention through their Home Mission Board provided many important services to the National Baptists not least of which were their assistance in helping them procure loans and mortgages, assisting with salaries for personnel in home mission work. The northern white churches, including the Baptists (and later the Southern Baptists as well), provided large amounts of monies for the founding and maintenance of black schools, a practice which they began immediately following the Civil War and which had become, by the end of the century, a kind of tradition — one that we contend militated against the development of rigorous independence on the part of the separate black denominations. From 1900 to 1915, R. H. Boyd's report of the Publishing Board to the National Baptist convention extended appreciation for the cooperation of the Southern Baptists, and subsequent reports fol-

lowed a similar pattern. See *the Journal of the 24th Annual Session of the National Baptist Convention held with the Ebenezer Third Baptist Church, Austin, Texas, September 14–19, 1904* (Nashville: National Baptist Publishing Board, 1904), 94ff. See also p. 97 for the "Articles of Agreement of Cooperation Between the Southern Baptist Home Mission Board and the National Baptist Convention." See also recommendation no. 1 (ibid., 31). It is important to note, however, that the nature of the cooperation was always that of whites providing the resources that blacks needed: never the reverse. It is also significant that most of the black church schools were and continue to be heavily dependent on the financial support of whites.

29. While the Martin Luther King, Jr., movement sought white financial support throughout its history, his was the first mass movement among blacks that succeeded in getting large numbers of whites (especially church people) existentially involved as participants for racial justice in the activities of direct nonviolent resistance.

30. Walls, *The African Methodist Episcopal Zion Church*, 493. See also W. A. Visser 't Hooft, ed., *The First Assembly of the World Council of Churches*, 216–17.

31. See Walls, *The African Methodist Episcopal Zion Church*, 486ff.

32. Ibid., 490.

33. Ibid., 490–91.

34. Wilmore, *Black Religion and Black Radicalism*, 69.

35. *Journal of the 42nd Annual Session of the National Baptist Convention held with the churches in St. Louis, Missouri, December 6–11, 1922* (Nashville: National Baptist Publishing Board, 1923), 51.

36. Ibid., 53.

37. Ibid.

38. Herbert Aptheker, ed., *A Documentary History of the Negro People in the United States* (New York: Citadel Press, 1964), 2:749.

3

Moral Agency in Conflict

PERSON-SOCIETY RELATIONSHIP

Persons are related to their sociopolitical context as parts are related to wholes. Neither has any existence apart from the other. Although they are mutually interdependent, they are not interchangeable, because the whole is greater than the sum of its parts, that is, the sociopolitical context is greater than the persons who comprise it. Persons are born into a ready-made world that constitutes the paramount conditions for human development. Specifically, those conditions designate the moral ethos of the society. They represent the society's most basic set of shared values that find significant expression in various communal symbols, rituals, pronouncements, celebrations, and the like. These values comprise the basic cultural paradigm in which the people find their sense of personal identity and group solidarity. Most important, however, that paradigm constitutes the society's ultimate source of authority for all moral obligation, legal enactment, social organization, and political association. In fact, no social or political advocacy can gain legitimacy in any society apart from an appeal, either implicitly or explicitly, to those paradigmatic values. Further, the specific political mission or "vocation" of every nation is integrally tied to and expressive of this value substratum.

One of the primary functions of parents, teachers, and various cultural institutions is moral education — guiding, training, and nurturing the young in knowing, obeying, and affirming the culture's basic values. Hence, moral education can never take place in a vacuum; rather, it takes place in relation to a set of normative values. Harmony occurs in the context of mutuality (1) between persons and the society when the values of the latter are experienced by the former as self-affirming, that is, as a source of nurture for the self-actualization of persons; and (2) between the society and persons when the values of the latter are supportive of those of the former, that is, when persons have a spirit of patriotism aimed at enhancing the power of the larger whole. Similarly, disharmony occurs whenever the values of the society are experienced by persons as alien to their well-being, and vice versa. Thus, whenever particular social groups — religious, ethnic, economic, and the like — stand in opposition to the basic societal values, they necessarily threaten the entire social order. Whether they view themselves as cultural reform groups or as thoroughgoing revolutionaries, they are inevitably perceived by the larger whole as radical, because their challenge impinges on the sacred grounding of the society itself. That has been the implicit danger in all moral reform groups, and especially in those activities of the black churches which are aimed at social change in race relations.

The moral implications of a sociopolitical context that restricts or prohibits the actualization of human potentiality are immense not only for the well-being of individuals but also for the integrity of the state. On the one hand, the state is denied the constructive contributions of those it rejects; on the other, it finds itself in a constant state of fear concerning its capacity to maintain its own position of privilege and control. Hence its growth in cultural richness is diminished proportionately. Since growth is the essence of life, the proscription of the other is, at the same time, self-restricting. But the greater hurt is nevertheless experienced by those who are excluded, since their loss is not merely quantitative but profoundly existential. Their humanity is threatened. Howard Thurman says it well:

> If there are any citizens within the state who by definition, stated or implied, are denied freedom of access to the resources of community as established within the state, such persons are assailed at the very foundation of their sense of belonging. . . . The term "second class citizen" is often used to describe such a status. This means that

such persons are "outsiders" living in the midst of "insiders,"
required to honor the same demands of sovereignty but denied the
basic rewards of sovereignty.[1]

The profound nature of the exclusion about which we are speaking cannot be grasped apart from an understanding of the integral
relationship between persons and society. Whenever persons are
rejected by society, the result is a loss of place; the result is exile.
Whenever a pattern of rejection persists from one generation to
another and is firmly rooted in an ideology, the rejected ones
become destined to a veritable permanent state of exile wherein
they have no sense of belonging, neither to the community nor to
the territory. Since it is necessary for persons to be nourished by
a communal eros in order to become fully human, an imposed
exile necessitates the formation of a substitute community, and, as
we have seen, that has been one of the major functions of the black
churches. Born and reared in an alien sociopolitical context, blacks
have had little hope for any sense of genuine national belonging.
All attempts at self-actualization on the part of both individuals
and the race as a whole have been plagued with many and varied
forms of social proscription, each of which has been based on a
particular understanding of the nature of black humanity along
with a corresponding institutionalized policy. For example, (1)
slavery was based on the view that blacks were subhuman and
hence needed to be owned and directed by others; (2) the American Colonization Society sought to repatriate this inferior race in
Africa, because it contended that whites would never accept them
as equals; (3) universal racial segregation and discrimination in the
South (similar to that which was long practiced in the North
toward the freemen) became the dominant social policy in the
twentieth century for expressing the doctrine of racial inequality;
(4) the legal demise of the Jim Crow system at mid-century has left
in place large-scale urban ghettoization which, in turn, ensures for
the foreseeable future the perpetuation of a racial underclass. All
of these policies were designed to thwart the progress of blacks in
all dimensions of their common life, and, perhaps worst of all, they
have contributed to a sense of low esteem that blacks frequently
have of themselves — a problem that the churches have sought tire-

lessly to correct. Once again Howard Thurman describes the problem well:

> The real evil of segregation is the imposition of self-rejection! It settles upon the individual a status which announces to all and sundry that he is of limited worth as a human being. It rings him round with a circle of shame and humiliation. It binds his children with a climate of no-accountness as a part of their earliest experience of the self. Thus it renders them cripples, often for the length and breadth of their days. And from this there is no forgiveness, only atonement. And only God can judge of what that atonement consists. What does it mean to grow up with a cheap self-estimate? There is a sentence I copied many years ago, the source of which I have forgotten: "We were despised so long at last we despised ourselves."[2]

But the self-denigration was never complete in spite of the countless individuals who "suffered unto death" every form of psychological and social damage. The survival of the race is attributable to two causes: (1) the resiliency of the human spirit to resist its own destruction either from within or from without; and (2) the social policies that forced the race into a state of dependency rather than total annihilation. The relationship of these two causes reveals a conflict at the heart of black America's moral self-understanding.

THE MORAL REALM

The moral dimension of life comprises one of the most distinctive differences between human beings and other animals. Morality is expressive of the capacity to determine the quality of human activity by making choices in accordance with understandings of good and bad, right and wrong. As moral agents, human beings are able to perceive others as subjects, and in their encounter with them they may choose to treat them either as subjects or as objects. Similarly, all human beings claim rights that obligate others to respect their dignity as subjects. Paul Tillich described this claim as the locus of the moral act per se. In fact, he argued that morality is born only in the act of treating the other as a person, since to do otherwise would be an objectification of the other: hence destruction of the other's personhood, and not only that but also a corresponding loss of the agent's own personhood. "Injustice against the other one is always injustice against oneself. The master who treats the slave not as an ego but as a thing endangers his own identity as an ego. The slave by his very existence hurts the master as much as he is hurt by him. The external inequality is balanced by the destruction of the ego-quality of the master."[3] The reciprocal activity of respecting persons constitutes the moral realm of human existence. In a cyclical way, however, the moral act itself constitutes the person as person. Becoming a person, a moral being, necessitates the treating of another as a person. In such an act, being and doing are interdependent. Hence, moral activity is always human activity in relation to other persons, either directly or indirectly. Thus it is a mistake to view morality as private if the latter implies social isolation.

At an early period, black Americans recognized the implications of a loss of morality, a loss of their humanity. In large part that is what motivated the race as a whole to resist every temptation to become habituated to hatred, bitterness, malice, vengeance. In that respect, blacks have always felt themselves to be the victors in a moral struggle. Nowhere in the literature of whites or blacks will one find wholesale typifications of blacks as a hostile race. On the contrary, the literature and folklore of whites have bequeathed to us such poignant symbols as the sensitive, affectionate "mammy" and the trustworthy, complacent "Uncle Tom" (to mention only two), both of which portray subservience in the spirit of love and loyalty. Although blacks have always reacted to such symbols with feelings ranging from ambivalence to outrage, they nevertheless have spoken of themselves customarily as loyal and faithful compatriots. In fact, like most conquered peoples, blacks have developed considerable ambivalence toward whites. Their high measure of appreciation for the power of their conquerors has often resulted, in turn, in the gradual development of a low estimation of themselves, especially in relation to those areas of life from which they had been excluded. But in keeping with the spirit of conquered peoples, blacks have never viewed whites as their moral superiors. Rather, they have considered them to be immoral at best and amoral at worst. Judgments based on the former implied that whites were capable of moral reform, but those based on the latter relegated them outside the moral realm altogether. In the main, blacks have tended to give credence to both points of view in spite of their apparent contradiction. That has resulted in developing, at best, an ambiguous understanding of the nature of the morality of whites: an understanding that has also presented them with a major challenge, namely, to develop and preserve among themselves a high standard of morality in both their individual and collective activities.

In the nineteenth century virtually all black leaders, ecclesiastical and otherwise, looked upon the slave experience as one of moral and social degradation. Consequently they assumed major responsibility for "uplifting" the race by means of moral education. It was hoped that such training would result in the development of black men and women of good moral character, solidly grounded in the virtues of industry, thrift, patience, and goodwill—virtues that they considered necessary for legitimating their claim for full and equal citizenship rights. It did not take long, however, before black leaders perceived that their struggle entailed the task not only of rehabilitating the race from the effects of an oppressive past but also of confronting a rapidly rising tide of racial segregation that was destined to shape race relations for the foreseeable future. Nevertheless they continued to give high priority to the moral improvement of the race.

Throughout the nineteenth century black religious leaders assumed that moral development was not possible apart from conversion to Christianity. That sentiment was not peculiar to them alone, but virtually pervaded the entire society, the secular as well as the religious realms. In an 1837 issue of the *Weekly Advocate*, later known as *The Colored American*, Monroe Fordham quoted the following: "The religion of the gospel is the only foundation of virtue . . . and if a man is unrestrained by religion, he is aloof from all moral restraint."[4] At the 1884 Centennial Methodist Conference in Baltimore, Bishop J. W. Hood of the African Methodist Episcopal Zion Church criticized the Protestant Episcopal Convention for its inability to make Christians of blacks in the South. In his judgment, the principal reason for such failure lay in their refusal to emphasize the importance of a radical conversion experience which alone he thought would have effected significant moral change. In the same speech he praised the effective efforts of Methodism in dealing with people of low and degraded status. The address readily reveals a definite class bias when he clearly states that the lower classes are not as mature as the middle classes and hence are unable to cope with the potential dangers implicit in drinking, dancing, and the like. The following excerpt reveals both the spirit and the content of the address which typified most of the social teaching of his time:

> Dr. Tucker, in his address to the Protestant Episcopal Convention, admitted the inability of that church to make Christians of the Negroes in the South. We are happy to say that Methodism has met no insurmountable difficulty in its efforts among that class. Nor is there any lack in the power of God's Word to reach them, low and degraded as they are. Nor is there any lack in their susceptibility to improvement. The lack is in the means employed. Dr. Tucker is a fair representative of the ministers of that Church who have labored among the freedom of the South. They expect to make Christians of them without a new birth. They expect to change the life without the change of heart. They seem to expect a pure stream without purifying the fountain. They seem to expect an evil tree to produce good fruit. It is no wonder that they have met disappointment. They discourage what they call extravagance and fanaticism and see no necessity for a radical change. They encourage dancing and other amusements, which, in themselves, may not be sinful, but because they were associated with the drunken, Christmas frolics in the slavery period, they were truly demoralizing to the freed-men. The fact is overlooked that cultured people can indulge in amusements without harm to themselves which might ruin others. Eating meat was no harm to Paul, but it might have caused some weak brother to stumble. . . . It is the height of folly to go to a long oppressed, deeply degraded, and grossly ignorant people, expecting to train them into righteousness in one generation without a complete putting off of the old man and putting on of the new man; old things must pass away, and all things become new. There must be a new birth and a new heart. Methodism recognizes this, and hence the abundant success where others have failed. . . . The only way to awaken the ignorant masses is by the powerful preaching of God's word, and the working of miracles in the souls of men by the power of the Holy Ghost.[5]

Needless to say, the view that morality and Christianity were synonymous was not distinctive among blacks but actually permeated the major institutions of the late nineteenth and the first half of the twentieth century. That was due in part to the immense impact that the revivalist movement has had on the nation. This movement sought moral and social reform through religious conversion. In that respect, the black churches reflected the general cultural ethos; the only difference was their goal, namely, the moral and social development of black Americans.

In harmony with that same revivalist social ethic that dominated their day, the black churches regularly issued moral pronouncements against alcoholic beverages, gambling, dancing, divorce, sexual promiscuity, and breaking the law. It was universally agreed among them that those vices militated against the race's moral and religious uplift. None doubted that the moral deficiency of the race had been caused by the conditions of three centuries of slavery imposed on it by white America. Also, few doubted that the development of good moral character on the part of blacks would constitute their passport to full and equal citizenship status. In other words, they believed implicitly that the moral degradation of the race had been caused by environmental factors, not by nature. Hence they were equally convinced that a change in those conditions through education and various kinds of social assistance would result in the type of moral formation in the race that would refute for all time the belief that blacks were by nature inferior to whites. It must be remembered, nevertheless, that their high degree of realism concerning the ignorance and moral degradation of the race as it emerged from slavery was no shield for the offense the black churches took toward those who held that the race was morally deficient by nature. The Quadrennial Address of the Bishops of the African Methodist Episcopal Church typified the responsive and protective posture of the church in relation to such sentiments.

> The race has been charged with ignorance, immorality, indifference and disregard for the marriage vow. . . . We deny the false and slanderous accusation against the virtue of our women and the manhood of our men and speak from personal knowledge of the moral

and social condition of the people, and affirm that the ideals of the
leaders of the people are as high as the ideal of life of their neigh-
bors, and that their practical life is more in harmony with the Ten
Commandments, the Golden Rule and the life of The Man of Sor-
rows and the humble Nazarene, than those who are bearing false
witness against their neighbor without any personal knowledge of
the charges alleged.[6]

As indicated in Bishop Hood's address, none were more convinced than the black Methodists that they had the key to the task
of converting grossly immoral people first to Christianity and
thence to an upright moral life. Obviously that conviction
stemmed from the tradition of the Wesleys, which began with a
focus on moral reform in the slums of London. Along with the
English Methodists, black Methodists also believed that the mission of Methodism was to all classes rather than to one alone. In
keeping with their practical outlook, both English and black
Methodists were certain that the only way to convert the upper
classes was to appeal to their sense of benevolent paternalism
toward the lower classes, a view that was clearly explicated in an
address by the Reverend J. W. Hamilton to the Centennial Methodist Conference entitled "The Mission of Methodism to the
Extremes of Society."[7] Similarly, the black churches in the late
nineteenth and early twentieth centuries believed without question in the virtues embodied in the upper classes of both races. In
fact, most believed that the sociopolitical salvation of blacks as a
race lay in the moral discernment and prudential acts of the white
upper class in alliance with the dedicated leaders of the black
upper class. One possible reason for this belief lay in the tradition
of the abolitionist movement which had been led by upper-class
whites in alliance with the blacks who were free before the Civil
War (this condition being the principal characteristic that distinguished the black upper class from the newly emancipated masses,
since at that time there was no black middle class). But the primary reason was that the progenitors of the black church independence movement in the nineteenth century were all members
of the black upper class which, by and large, modeled itself after
the white upper class. Both races viewed their upper-class status

as a mark of privilege which, unlike the middle classes of the early twentieth century, preferred to be characterized not as entrepreneurs but as exemplars of cultural refinement in morals, tastes, and manners. More important, they understood themselves to be under obligation to bear special responsibility for the welfare of the larger social organism through dedicated works of charity as well as social, moral, and political reform. In short, they viewed themselves as social leaders with a mission to shape the society in accordance with their moral vision. Thus it is not surprising that they exhibited a benevolent paternalism toward the society as a whole, and black religious leaders assumed a similar posture toward their race. Let us hasten to add that this does not imply a pejorative relationship but, on the contrary, one in which the churches took upon themselves a dual leadership role: (1) to protect and defend the race against the onslaughts of racism and (2) to "uplift" the race from the moral degradation of slavery. The former implied reactive functions in relation to the larger society, while the latter implied constructive and developmental functions aimed at racial development.

Not only the clergy but also the lay members of the black churches identified with the upper-class ethos. This is clearly seen in many places, but especially in the work of Nannie Burroughs, one of the great leaders of the Women's Auxiliary of the National Baptist Convention for over seven decades. Throughout that time she labored for the development and maintenance of the Women's Industrial Training School in Washington, D.C. One of the chief aims of that school was to train black women in the domestic arts not only to be more effective wage earners but also to learn how to rear children dedicated to the task of race leadership. Hence that goal necessitated adequate training in speech, deportment, and moral virtue. Ms. Burroughs used the term "race servants" to specify that goal. "It is necessary to teach our young people to know from the very start of their school life that they are being trained to become servants of their race."[8]

That tradition of the black upper class was what inspired W. E. B. DuBois to construct a quasi-sociological category which he called "the talented tenth" — that portion of the population in any group which comprises the leadership class, distinguished by its education and refined tastes,, and embued with a mission to enhance the quality of the social order. These were thought to be the scholars, educators, ministers, lawyers, and political leaders. Following World War I, however, black leaders began to worry because they saw the nascent rise of a new class, "the black middle class," uncommitted to race leadership as the paramount goal and dedicated instead to a self-serving utilitarian ethic rooted in such values as individualism, moneymaking, and conspicuous consumption.[9] This phenomenon was especially troubling to the black churches and was regularly scoffed at in sermons and pronouncements. Thus for many decades following emancipation the black churches believed that destiny had bestowed upon them a special mission. They accepted this mission as a formidable challenge because they felt themselves charged with the task of bringing the race up (educationally, morally, economically, socially) out of ignorance and degradation to a desired state that would virtually be the envy of all white Americans. They were optimistic in spite of the many obstacles that confronted them. They shouldered the responsibility with religious fervor and fought battles against the evils of racial injustice and prejudice with as much zeal (if not might) as ever characterized the Crusades of the late Middle Ages, the Reformers of the sixteenth and seventeenth centuries, and the Revivalists of the eighteenth and nineteenth centuries. They believed that theirs was a religious cause and that God was on their side. They took pride in their annual assessments of how far the race had come and never doubted that the final victory would be theirs since their cause was just and their commitment to it was firm. The sentiment of the 1908 Quadrennial Address typified that spirit: "Because of early disadvantages, the race was and is destined to struggle. Progress will be made and the race will rise."[10]

EDUCATION, ECONOMICS, CIVIL RIGHTS

In the 1896 Quadrennial Address of the African Methodist Episcopal Church the bishops presented a list of the things that the churches should do, and that list had the stamp of tradition on it. In other words, it represented then, as it does now, those activities on which the black churches have always maintained a broad consensus. A partial list follows:

    II. To encourage the organization of the social efforts, the Mutual Aid, Benevolent and Christian efforts of the Race.

    III. To support the Commercial, Agricultural and Financial efforts of the Race. . . .

    VI. To give an opportunity to show by example what is possible for the Negro to do for himself and others. . . .

    VII. To stand as a living protest against caste in the church, at the Sacramental table and in the Ministry. . . .

    XI. To increase in the young men and women Race Pride.

       1. By preserving the biographies of men of the Race.

       2. By showing that we need not be ashamed of our origin and ancestry.

       3. By showing that originally the Negroes were the Leaders of Civilization.

       4. That they were among the most active promoters of Christianity.

       5. That our night of bondage has never been without the star of hope. . . .

    XV. We are to furnish the race with an anchor of hope that they can cast into the deepest sea and which will hold until every son and daughter of Adam has secured his equal political and social rights.[11]

Since slaves had been denied formal education of any sort, universal illiteracy characterized the masses of blacks as they greeted the Emancipation Act. The churches immediately sought to remedy that condition by founding schools and allying with both northern philanthropists[12] and white churches to alter this severely crippling social condition. By the turn of the century both the black Methodists and the black Baptists credited themselves with having had no little hand in reversing the situation to a veritable state of literacy in less than thirty years. All hoped that such a rapid change would be encouragement to the race's friends and proof to its enemies that whenever the measure of quality is intelligence, industry, and dedication, blacks are second to none.

The black churches long believed that the education of blacks was not a mere end in itself, but instead a means for changing white public opinion about blacks. All believed that if whites would see more and more blacks embodying gentle manners, excellence in speech, good moral character, industry, and good-will, they would cease stereotyping blacks according to the boister-ous behavior of the black masses. The minutes of the women's conventions from 1900–1920 are replete with attacks on the con-duct of the masses and its negative impact on the race as a whole. The conventions sought effective means of reforming the public behavior of the masses. This attitude permeated the black commu-nity's upper class. Black newspapers zealously crusaded against the black masses. Throughout the first half of the twentieth cen-tury the cartoons in those papers regularly depicted the conduct of the lower classes in satirical form, for example, loud talking, unbecoming conduct in public places, laziness, parading in the streets, drunkenness, sexual promiscuity, wayward women, and a host of similar vices. Preachers frequently drew upon anecdotes, metaphors, and gestures that vividly portrayed the contrasting behavior of lower- and upper-class blacks.

In addition, the black churches have believed that the task of racial uplift (educationally and morally) lay basically in the hands of blacks themselves, and consequently their schools became the prime exemplars of that viewpoint. The schools, moreover, con-tained the ground of hope for blacks, and each commencement exercise engendered in the people a feeling that things were getting better. Both of these attitudes are reflected in Bishop Tanner's response to the view that neither the North nor the South would elevate the race.

> No man or community of men can elevate another. Elevation must always come from within. What the North and the South, however, can do is to cease their injustices, direct and indirect, and allow the Negro to elevate himself. If, however, they had continued their opposition, it would have been impossible for him to have acquitted himself as he has done, is doing, and gives promise of. Things, how-ever, are moving on all right. The little remaining opposition can be overcome, and another generation will make croaking more nonsen-sical than it is now.[13]

It was generally agreed among the black churches that the eco-nomic standing of the race was directly proportional to the level of educational and moral development. Hence they believed that improvement in the latter would result in a corresponding improvement in the former. Although many black economic enterprises had their beginnings in the black churches, and although the churches themselves constituted major economic institutions, they never gave high institutional priority to black economic development. Hence the churches expended must less energy in that sphere of their life than in education, moral training, and civil rights. The reasons for this are certainly multiple, but a major one is that blacks viewed education and civil rights as necessary conditions for economic development. To combat racial discrimination and segregation in education, the black churches established a variety of schools, many of which were partially supported by monies from white churches and liberal philanthropists. Several of those schools continue, a few of the most prominent being Lane College (Christian Methodist Episcopal), Wilberforce University (African Methodist Episcopal), Livingstone College (African Methodist Episcopal Zion), American Baptist College of the Bible in the South (National Baptist Convention, U.S.A., Inc.). Each of these schools comprised a theological seminary as well. Training schools have also been sponsored by the churches, the most notable being the Women's Industrial Training School (National Baptist Convention, U.S.A., Inc.). Following the Civil War, scores of schools and colleges opened in the South under the auspices of state legislatures, the American Missionary Society, the Freeman's Bureau, and various white denominations. According to Bishop Gaines's writing in 1890:

> The most reliable statistics concerning the education of the race are those from the last census, and out of that we find that the Negro race in the United States has 17,822 schools, with 16,865 teachers. There has been great increase since then, as the census of the present year will show.[14]

It is important to note that Booker T. Washington's experiment at Tuskegee Institute and his famous address at the Atlanta Exposition in 1895 demonstrated in thought and practice how education could be harnessed for the economic development of the race under the conditions of restrictive civil rights. As already indicated, his program received the strong endorsement of the churches, as did the alternative view of education advocated by Washington's adversary, W. E. B. DuBois.[15]

Since the hostility of white America toward blacks has been so persistently pervasive, opposition to it inevitably became an important part of the agenda of all black organizations, beginning with the churches from the earliest times to the present day. It is no understatement to say that most black organizations have defined themselves largely in terms of that struggle. The psychological impact of racism on blacks was so great that during much of the nineteenth and early twentieth centuries the term "manhood Christianity" became a major sociological and religious symbol for them. It served to prove something not only to whites but to blacks as well. Blacks had been told for so many generations that they were an inferior race that many had become vulnerable to believing it themselves. This danger must have constituted the ultimate threat to the churches, since a belief in one's own inferiority inevitably must lead to such a state of demoralization that change is virtually rendered impossible. Thus the racial struggle had to be waged not only against the racism of white America per se but also against the tendencies within the race to believe racist propaganda. The latter function has always been correlated closely with the cultivation of the twin values of self-reliance and self-respect, both of which are exemplified in the development, maintenance, and improvement of religious institutions. The circularity of this argument specifies the integral relationship of the psychological and social dimensions of human existence.

Although the churches thought that ignorance, poverty, and moral degradation were the principal obstacles to racial advance during the latter part of the nineteenth century and to the end of World War I, all were thought to be caused by the larger problem, namely, racism in the form of restrictive civil rights. In fact, the churches believed that the entire plight of black Americans was caused either directly or indirectly by white America's denial of full and equal citizenship rights to the race. Nearly every church convention and conference deplored the social injustice perpetrated on blacks and issued resolutions and letters to the president and Congress of the United States[16] and set up special study commissions. Early in their history, the churches perceived that the so-called "Negro problem" was a misnomer, one that they corrected by calling it "America's problem," an understanding that was fully accepted by Gunnar Myrdal in his classic *An American Dilemma.*

The churches exhibited, however, a measure of ambiguity with respect to the question of civil rights. On the one hand, they believed that the civil rights of blacks would be respected after blacks proved that they were capable of being upright citizens of moral virtue and capable of high educational attainment as evidenced in demonstrated political, religious, and economic leadership. On the other hand, the churches were constantly puzzled over white America's seemingly blatant disregard of all such empirical evidence—for example, its persistence in treating blacks unfairly in the law courts and in giving them unequal service for equal fares on the trains and buses, to mention only two of a long list of racial grievances. This dilemma expressed one dimension of the general problem that blacks have had in relation to America and their place in it, the horns of which repeatedly appeared in the black churches in the form of: (1) those who advocated racial self-development as a means to the final goal of full and equal citizenship rights; (2) those who severely criticized America's injustice and hypocrisy as irredeemable and consequently advocated a more permanent form of racial separation. The former disposition, however, has dominated the life and thought of the black churches up to the present day even though it has had to defend itself constantly against the judgments of the latter.

Thus we contend that the moral leadership of the black churches has focused principally on the task of creating a sociopsychological support system for all endeavors of the race aimed at mutual aid, self-help programs, commercial enterprises, civil rights, race pride, education, and lawful protests against racism. Both the historical forms of racism and the responses of the black churches to them were splendidly summarized in "The Annual American Negro Keynote Address" delivered by the Reverend James Bryant of Atlanta at the 1921 National Baptist Convention.

The South has tried unsuccessfully (1) Slavery; (2) Domination; (3) Mob Violence; (4) Disfranchisement; (5) Ku Klux Klan or White Superiority and Supremacy. . . . The North has tried (1) Discrimination; (2) Segregation; (3) Starvation or Non-Employment; (4) Prevarication in Politics to no avail. Some of both sections have advocated (1) Emigration; (2) Segregation; (3) Miscegenation; (4) Subordination; (5) Annihilation; (6) Migration. But still like Banquo's Ghost the problem will not die.

The Negro has tried (1) Religion; (2) Education; (3) Acquisition of property; (4) Participation in diversified business; (5) Toleration of submission under protest. . . . There can be, there will be, there ought not be any permanent solution of our human problem until all men regardless of race, color or nation will acknowledge in theory and practice the Fatherhood of God, the brotherhood of man, the equality of the human race, and the Golden Rule as the universal law and conduct in all our relationships as man with man.

(1) Such a course will guarantee absolute freedom and equality before God and under the law of men.
(2) Symmetrical education to all our youth.
(3) Impartial participation in all affairs of government.
(4) Civil and political equality to the private citizen as well as the professional politician.
(5) Social justice and equality, but not social intermingling, nor intermarriage.

Each race group in its solidarity, individuality and separation has a distinct contribution to make to the civilization and Christianization of the world.[17]

Bryant then set forth his advice to the race, which contained all the moral admonitions embedded in the black church tradition.

A Plain Statement to my people whether North or South.
1. Remember there is no superiority nor inferiority in the mere accident of color; character and not color makes men.
2. Minimize mere appearance and maximize sterling character.
3. Resolve and strive to be producers and not consumers, assets and not liabilities in the community in which you live and the country of which you are a part.
4. Take life seriously. Work and not play only.
5. Think, don't feel your way. Be controlled by your thought, and not by your feelings.

6. Pay your taxes regularly; register always; vote in all elections.
7. Seek and plan interracial fellowship and cooperation on righteous, equitable and manly basis.
8. Innoculate yourself and your children with race respect and race pride.[18]

The churches have always affirmed the need for new and continued support of all initiatives exercised in any of these eight areas, and from time to time they themselves have spearheaded such efforts which often served as models for other groups. Curiously, however, effectiveness has not been the chief goal of the black churches in any of their activities. Suffice it to say that in their perspective, the process of initiating activities and lending their unqualified support to other blacks desirous of similar goals has intrinsic worth in itself. In that respect, the churches have not been guided by a narrow utilitarian ethic. Rather, they have viewed their activities as having intrinsic worth quite apart from their consequences. Such an orientation to value inevitably dispels all fears of failure, and that is a major refuge for oppressed peoples who are all too familiar with failure. We do not wish to imply, of course, that the churches did not desire their activities to result in effective social change; we merely wish to point out that the successful accomplishment of that goal has not been the only measure of value for them. Rather, the spirits of blacks have always been touched by a latent sense of victory attending the satisfaction they experience from the activities themselves. Thus Martin Luther King, Jr., spoke out of the tradition when he asserted that nonviolent resistance was redemptive in itself, whether or not the desired goal was realized.

MORAL CONFLICT

A traditional conflict in the moral thought of the black churches has centered on dual loyalty to the functions of (1) serving the needs of the race and (2) serving the Lord of the church. On the one hand, black churches have been race institutions, always working in the interest of the race by preaching freedom, civil rights, temperance, and industry. On the other hand, however, the churches have been religious institutions with a strong sense of obligation to be faithful to the Redeemer, whom they worshiped as the source of ultimate truth and whose eschatological vision they employed as their criterion for social criticism. In the minds of the black churches, aggressive action in behalf of justice has always been tantamount to serving the needs of the race. Similarly, zealous action in behalf of truth has traditionally characterized the nature of their preaching and worship, the substance of which has been for them the source of social justice. In other words, they have viewed justice, improving the quality of the race's life, as grounded in truth, that is, in the will of the Redeemer. Trust in the latter as well as in God's final compensatory action of redeeming the world has always comprised the focus of their internal religious activity and, by implication, justified those external religious activities aimed at racial justice.

The tendency of the black churches has been to employ the thought patterns of the white churches in articulating their theological understandings. Whenever called upon to justify their social reform activities, they have had no difficulty appealing to those common theological understandings. But in the main, black churches have seen no need for sustained theological and ethical reflection that might lead to the development of a systematic body of thought. Certainly the absence of research scholars in their service contributed in large part to the dirth of such constructive and critical thought. Moreover, by affirming the basic theology of the white churches, the black churches have failed to see the disservice they rendered themselves, since the thought patterns of the white churches were not always commensurate with the activities of the black churches, especially those pertaining to the embodiment of racial justice. Further, apart from preaching, the black churches have given little importance to the systematic explication of their social thought. Since little sustained effort has been made in the black churches toward preserving the content of sermons and critically analyzing them, much of the creative social thought is available to us only in fragments. Hence scholars of the black churches are dependent on the primary materials arising out of the internal life of the organizations wherein the accumulated knowledge and wisdom are largely implicit.

Unfortunately the black churches also failed to perceive that ecclesiastical theology necessarily arises out of the activities of the churches and not vice versa. Hence their judgment was in error that those white churches which excluded blacks from participation were willfully distorting the known truth of the gospel. They had failed to discern that the theology of those churches was shaped by their actions, and that the two were compatible. In other words, they failed to discern that practice is prior to thought in the order of theological and ethical reflection.

Contrary to the general opinion among blacks, white America experienced no dilemma between its theological thought and the way it treated blacks. For white America it was not a matter of believing in true justice while practicing injustice. Rather, in that respect, the white churches actually experienced no alienation between their thought and practice. This is evidenced by the fact that any attempt to preach racial equality in the pulpits of white churches has always been viewed as an act of hostility against their prevailing ethos. Since blacks assumed a static theology that transcended both races, they inevitably concluded that racist activities were deliberate violations of professed theological beliefs. They had forgotten that the Christian churches ostensibly had no difficulty with slavery for centuries prior to the abolitionism of the nineteenth century. In fact, it is highly doubtful that the New Testament itself offers unequivocal opposition to slavery. Thus, if slavery had such a long history among Christians, one should not suppose that Christians would necessarily believe themselves to be under religious obligation to treat ex-slaves as first-class citizens.

Because blacks believed implicitly in the rightness of their opposition to racism, they felt no real need to justify that activity by ethical arguments. When they engaged in such arguments it was usually for the purpose of putting whites on the defensive; and that, incidentally, has always been a strategic weapon that black preachers held for reserve use, especially when speaking to racially mixed congregations. Capacity to use it well continues to constitute a major attribute of good preaching in the black community. Unfortunately, however, blacks have severely hindered their own thought by their misunderstanding of the relationship of morality and theology. Because they believed that morality was derived from theology, and that theology was a fixed certainty for all Christians, they have been slow in making a creative contribution to theological thought. They found themselves instead on the horns of a dilemma where they accepted wholesale the theology of the white churches and used it in the service of fighting racism. This is ironic, because the black church independence movement was a deliberate effort to separate itself from the white churches in order to express the biblical understanding of humanity more truly, to worship more faithfully, and to serve the needs of the race more diligently. Yet the movement failed to see the irony implied in its inability to discern that racism inhered in the theological thought as well as in the practices of the white churches, since the two were integrally related. Thus an unconscious dilemma existed which acted in many ways as a serious constraint on the theological understandings of blacks. Although black preachers displayed infinite creativity in the use of the imagination for rhetorical purposes, and although their sermons comprised a reservoir for theological construction, no critical, systematic theology of the black experience emerged until the dawn of black theology in the late 1960s. Thus it appears that the artistry of preaching, music, and song expressed the intellectual power of the black churches more than the literary word. This judgment implies an indictment of those few black schools of religion that failed to encourage significant critical research on the thought and practice of the black churches.

As we have seen, the black churches have a notable history of founding educational institutions and promoting learning both within and outside the church. Closely associated with the educational programs of the respective churches, black denominational publishing houses were founded to enable black writers to participate in the production of study materials and to protect the children and laity from being exposed, either implicitly or explicitly, to racist propaganda. The publishing houses also provided an avenue for the publication of monographs by blacks about blacks and especially historical studies of the churches and their leaders. As the progenitors of the black secular press, they constituted for many decades one of the race's chief means of gaining information along with editorialized comments on issues pertaining to the welfare of the race. With some notable exceptions, however, these agencies also failed to give adequate encouragement and support to the constructive development of black theological and ethical thought.[19] The church school materials followed basic lectionary patterns and relied on standard commentaries for biblical exegesis. The task of the black writer was that of applying the material in as relevant a way as possible to a black constituency. This was usually accomplished by illustrating the message in the context of the black experience. Thus, in spite of the ready constituency in the black church schools, the technical facilities of the publishing houses, and the racist stereotypes that pervaded the larger society regarding the inferiority of blacks and their concomitant social status in the society, the study materials of the black churches have been singularly unimpressive according to most measures of imagination and creativity. An immense potentiality has been unrealized mainly because blacks failed to attend critically to the nature of the thought that guided their activities. Consequently, the theology that characterizes the masses of black churches has been closely akin to orthodox Christian conservatism buttressed by a literalistic view of the Bible. But the narrow legalism implied by such a theology in the white community has usually been softened by the realities of life in the black community as well as the imaginative liberties that preachers have customarily taken in "expounding the text." Curiously, the latter appears to have had little influence on the content of the published study materials. This may in part be attributable to the social gap that has separated the oral and written traditions in the black community, the oral having always been dominant in the black churches. Those learned clergy who were educated in white seminaries tended to reflect the liberal theological ethos and the corresponding social attitudes that characterized those colleges which permitted blacks to enroll.

The moral dilemma as illustrated in the educational and publishing tasks of the black churches has also been vividly present in foreign mission programs. Early in their history the black churches discovered the neglect of Africa on the part of white foreign mission boards. In that awareness they quickly moved to fill the void in the interest of treating Africa justly and in accordance with their firm belief that they were better qualified to take the gospel to Africa than were whites. Further, in their efforts to model themselves as closely as possible after their white denominational counterparts, they sought opportunities to enter the foreign mission enterprise. The neglect of Africa presented the opportunity they needed to demonstrate another dimension of their leadership capacity. By taking this opportunity, they found a means of identifying with Western Christian superiority both in its religion and in its civilization. Consequently, a major impetus for their involvement in foreign missions was to help civilize Africa, which they thought would contribute significantly to racial uplift both symbolically and politically. We see here a striking similarity between the task of bringing up the race from the degradation of slavery and that of bringing Africa out of "heathenism" and "uncivilized" culture. The theological and ethical substance of their foreign mission enterprise thus differed little from that of their white counterparts.

In their efforts to maintain their humanity by resisting the dehumanizing efforts of racism, the black churches found themselves engulfed in a sea of moral conflicts that pervaded their thought and action regarding intraracial and interracial matters. The absence of continuous critical thought about their mission ensured the perpetuation of traditional understandings and practice, and they often failed to see that both their thought and action were shaped within the framework of that which the larger white society found acceptable. Further, their opposition to the forms of absolute racial separation, as advocated by those who identify with the tradition of black nationalism, hindered them from discerning clearly the wisdom of combining these motions in order to justify and promote what in fact they had become — practitioners of a racial pluralism that shunned both wholesale assimilationism and racial separatism. Racial pluralism seeks to embody racial assimilation and racial separation in a dynamic and creative equilibrium. Although such a pluralistic concept might have been premature for the times, it nevertheless explains well what the black churches had become. Their many and varied moral conflicts were largely the product of this unresolved problem.

Finally, it must be noted that one important locus of considerable social criticism in the black denominations was the women's organizations which often caused the official denominational leaders more than a little consternation. Time and again the women kept specific issues of racial injustice alive that were otherwise concealed in the generalized rhetoric of those occupying the highest positions of power and authority. In the early years of the National Baptist conventions the official records indicate that the women appeared to be more concerned than the men about the blatant unfairness evidenced in the issue of equal fares and unequal treatment for blacks and whites on the trains — basic inconveniences such as the lack of assistance for blacks in getting on and off trains, the absence of the stepping-stool in ascending and descending the black passenger cars, the indignity implied by one bathroom in the black sections that had to be shared by both men and women, the lack of any concessions for either food or drinks in the segregated cars — to mention only a few. The women repeatedly raised these and other issues in their meetings and tried, with considerable difficulty, to mobilize some effective action. Further, the women appeared to be more daring than the men in bringing controversial figures such as Booker T. Washington and W. E. B. DuBois (as well as many others) to their assemblies long before the denominations were willing to grant official sponsorship. Needless to say, a full-scale study is needed concerning the role and function of women as an active force for change both within and without the black denominations.

NOTES

1. Howard Thurman, *The Search for Common Ground* (New York: Harper & Row, 1971), 86–87.

2. Howard Thurman, *The Luminous Darkness: A Personal Interpreta-*

tion of the Anatomy of Segregation and the Ground of Hope (New York: Harper & Row, 1965), 24.

3. Paul Tillich, *Love, Power and Justice* (New York: Oxford University Press, 1960), 78–79.

4. Monroe Fordham, *Major Themes in Northern Black Religious Thought, 1800–1860* (New York: Exposition Press, 1975), 35.

5. H. K. Carroll, W. P. Harrison, J. H. Bayliss, eds., *Proceedings, Sermons, Essays and Addresses of the Centennial Methodist Conference held in the Mount Vernon Place Methodist Episcopal Church, Baltimore, Md., December 9–17, 1884* (New York: Phillips and Hunt, 1885), 478.

6. *Journal of the 20th Quadrennial Session of the General Conference of the African Methodist Episcopal Church*, Wilmington, N.C., May 4–22, 1896, 66.

7. Ibid., 529.

8. *Journal of the Twentieth Annual Session of the National Baptist Convention held in the Fifth Street Baptist Church, Richmond, Virginia, September 12–17, 1900* (Nashville: National Baptist Publishing Board, 1903), 312.

9. See E. Franklin Frazier's *Black Bourgeoisie* (New York: Free Press, 1957) for one of the earliest treatises on this phenomenon.

10. *Journal of the 23rd Quadrennial Session of the General Conference of the African Methodist Episcopal Church*, Norfolk, Virginia, May 24–31, 1908, 55.

11. *Journal of the 20th Quadrennial Session of the General Conference of the African Methodist Episcopal Church*, Wilmington, N.C., May 4–22, 1896, 98–99.

12. At the turn of the century such names as Peabody, Arthington, Slater, and Hand were well known among the churches for the aid they gave to the advance of black education.

13. Wesley J. Gaines, *African Methodism in the South; or, Twenty-five Years of Freedom* (Chicago: Afro-Am Press, 1969), 281.

14. Ibid.

15. The fact that Booker T. Washington's thought and program had strong support among the black churches is evidenced by his regular addresses to the National Baptist convention each year from 1903 onward. So regular was his attendance and so respected were his addresses that the convention called the Friday evening session the Booker T. Washington Night and that has continued up to the present day. In 1907 the minutes reported that Washington had given the best lecture ever delivered at the convention. (see *Journal of the 27th Annual Session of the National Baptist Convention held with the Metropolitan Baptist Church, Washington, D.C., December 11–16, 1907* [Nashville: National Baptist Publishing Board, 1908], 95). In 1909 the convention denied two newspaper reports stating that Booker T. Washington had been barred because of his views

by formally endorsing him and his program (see *Journal of the 29th Annual Session of the National Baptist Convention held with the Baptist Churches of Columbus, Ohio, September 15-20, 1909* [Nashville: Baptist Publishing House, 1910], 174). In 1907 the convention dedicated the Women's Industrial School founded by the Women's Auxiliary Convention — an idea conceived nearly a decade earlier by M. Nannie Burroughs and strongly reflective of the Washington philosophy and program. It must also be said, lest one think this convention too ideological, that W. E. B. DuBois was invited many times as well to address the convention. Similarly, both men frequently addressed the Methodist conferences of the A.M.E. Church and the A.M.E. Zion Church.

16. It must be said, however, that most of those communiqués from the end of Reconstruction up to the 1930s were sent to the president of the United States because blacks felt that they had no other representation in the government, having been disfranchised in the South, their major population base.

17. *Journal of the 41st Annual Session of the National Baptist Convention, U.S.A., Inc., held with the Baptist churches in New Orleans, Louisiana, 1921* (Nashville: National Baptist Publishing Board, 1921), 232–33.

18. Ibid., 233–34.

19. *The Christian Recorder* of the A.M.E. Church must be viewed here as an exception, at least in its early history. It had been founded in 1854 to be a forum for the social ideas of black Americans, interpreting economic, social, political, and educational perspectives of the black leadership class. Religion, morality, science, and literature were all relevant subjects. After the Civil War the paper focused almost entirely on disseminating information to blacks concerning their rights, the effect of the law on the black community, to circulate petitions about race grievances, solicitations of financial support for testing the constitutionality of Jim Crow laws, urging blacks to be active in boycotts and voting. In the 1880s Bishop Tanner became the founder of *The Christian Review*, a quarterly journal that he thought would enable intellectuals to express themselves better. He aimed at publishing the best thoughts of the race and invited the participation of all — not just members of the A.M.E. Church. The Quarterly Review of the A.M.E. Zion Church was founded for similar purposes.

4

Political Wisdom in Deficiency

At the risk of repetition, let us begin this chapter with a summary statement concerning the conditions of black existence that are implied in our analysis thus far. This will enable us to advance our argument from a different vantage point.

In the perspective of black Americans, racism has been the bedrock of the American republic, shaping all dimensions of its political, economic, and social order. Paradoxically, blacks as a group have always had faith in the dream that racial justice would eventually be realized in this land. This curious fact seems incredible when the nature of their experience is considered: brought involuntarily to these shores by the violence of the slave trade; held in captivity for three centuries solely for the economic benefit of their white masters; reluctantly emancipated following a bitter civil war to face continuous threats of mob violence, disfranchisement, job discrimination, social segregation, and every possible form of personal and civil abuse. Hence one rightly inquires about the grounds upon which they based their hopes for racial justice. Our judgment that they actually had very little empirical bases for these hopes is rooted in a number of generalizations concerning this confused sense of communal and national identity.

In the first place, the American slave system was very effective in systematically stripping blacks of every vestige of cultural continuity with their native Africa. Unlike the vast majority of voluntary immigrants to this country, blacks soon found themselves alone in the world, with no genuine place of belonging either retrospectively or prospectively. Slavery had alienated them from their African past and emancipation had bequeathed to them the legacy of being indelibly marked as undesirable citizens. Out of ignorance they tended to adopt the prevailing understandings of Africa as a land of savages. Furthermore, constant opposition to the racist ideology that conditioned their existence in America caused them to doubt increasingly the moral integrity of the larger society. Estranged from Africa and rejected by America, blacks were deprived of the two most basic existential conditions of life: a prideful place of origin and a firm sense of belonging. Hence they had an abiding sense of insecurity as they continued to hope either for a home in America in spite of their traditional exclusion or for the reestablishment of roots in Africa from which they had been culturally separated for more than three centuries. It is not surprising, therefore, that considerable ambiguity has character-ized their attitudes toward Africa, white America, and even black America.

Refusing to conceive of racial independence as a viable potential for racial self-sufficiency and not persuaded that colonization in Africa or elsewhere was a viable alternative, blacks found them-selves with no real option apart from commitment to an ideal hope that one day complete racial justice would be realized in America — a hope that had both religious and political significance. Reli-giously, this hope was rooted in the belief that perfect justice is promised in the kingdom of God, the eschatological vision. Politi-cally, it was grounded in the conviction that those who framed the American Constitution intended that it should specify and protect the rights of all citizens regardless of race, color, or creed. The dif-ference between the religious and political views lay in the fact that the first was grounded in an unshakable eschatological faith that admitted no uncertainty, while the latter was rooted in a political document that served the race as an unfulfilled promise. For the most part, however, blacks tended to unite their eschato-logical and political visions, whereby political realism was sub-sumed into political idealism. We shall return to this point later. Suffice it to say that the general locus of their political vision was

America even though from time to time they lost faith in that vision and in its stead substituted Africa — sometimes as symbol, other times as intentional goal, always with ambivalence.

Second, since identification with African culture was forcibly transferred to that of America, blacks eventually came to embody the substance of American culture as fully as white Americans.[1] But, as we have seen, they differed from whites in their rejection of all racist expressions of that substance. Thus it is surprising that white America's oppression of blacks is, in large part, a form of self-denial, because, in spite of their different circumstances, black and white Americans share all of the society's fundamental values pertaining to individualism, capitalism, democracy, private property, liberty, freedom of speech and worship, and views of marriage and the family, to mention only a few. Further, black and white Americans share most of the society's conventional behavior patterns. Clearly, white America's domination of all aspects of black America's existence has resulted in the latter's assimilation of the other's values, most of which have been promulgated regularly in black schools, colleges, businesses, social clubs, churches, families, and the like. Yet throughout the black community the dominant moral value that has made all the difference between the races has been their persistent resistance to racism as a fundamental condition of their existence. For various reasons, the black independent churches provided a more fertile context than any other organized effort for the cultivation of that orientation.

Moreover, black Americans have never thought of freedom, justice, civil rights, racial equality, and the like, as abstract principles, but rather as necessary conditions for human experience. Conversely, they have viewed the privation of such conditions as dehumanizing. Consequently their resistance to racial proscription (among other things) affirmed their humanity, since that activity alone embued them with self-respect and human dignity. In fact, the existence of black churches themselves evidenced their humanity in the most basic way, because in those places they experienced a public racial forum for addressing the fundamental issues pertaining to racial freedom, independence, and justice.

FREEDOM, INDEPENDENCE, AND
RACIAL JUSTICE

As already indicated, the black churches came into existence for the purpose of providing a space in which the race could experience freedom and develop those civic virtues which were denied them in the larger society. The black churches also hoped that their demonstrated capacities in building institutions and in developing the race would eventually cause whites to admit their errors by turning away from their former practices in favor of granting them all the rights and privileges of first-class citizenship.

Our contention has been that the black church independence movement began as a religious, moral, and political thrust for independence, freedom, and justice in the sanctuary of God, in the inner life of the individual, and in the society at large. We contend, further, that considerable success was soon achieved in the first two arenas (namely, the sanctuary of God and the inner life of the individual), but very little substantial progress has ever been realized in effecting racial justice in the larger society in spite of the various changes that have taken place in it. That is to say, the churches initially aimed at the political transformation of the larger society through the moral and religious development of the race. The inevitable concentration of the churches' activities on the latter often resulted in a de facto competition between their internal and external activities — internal institutional matters versus the wider public goal of racial justice. We must hasten to say, however, that although many local churches have succumbed from time to time to that temptation, none of the black denominations ever completely lost sight of the relationship of their twofold purpose of racial development and societal transformation. As the denominations grew in size and complexity, enormous amounts of time and energy were required of a limited number of competent leaders for institutional maintenance functions of buying and managing property, raising budgets, constructing buildings, directing expansion and the like, not to mention the more specific activities of founding churches, schools, publishing houses, and foreign mission fields (all of which were seen as necessary functions of the nascent denominations). In addition, these same leaders had to devote much time and energy to the worship and preaching functions of the churches, including the task of moral development by means of numerous oral and written exhortations against drinking, smoking, gambling, sexual promiscuity, dancing, divorce, and crime.[2] It is not hard to imagine how the internal focus on ecclesiastical and moral development could yield the desired results more readily than activity in the wider public domain, and that fact must have constantly tempted the church leaders to forsake the latter in favor of the former.

In spite of evidence to the contrary, the denominations have remained faithful to the founders of their respective traditions, who chose institutional separation from the white churches not as an end in itself, but as a means to the goal of enjoying freedom and justice in the larger society. As these founders were driven by the forces of racism to form their own churches, they were also forced to establish their own schools, colleges, publishing houses, and foreign mission programs in order to counteract the debilitating impact of racism. In the early years these necessary activities inevitably became institutional priorities which, over a period of time, tended to take on the mark of tradition and thus become impervious to change. But these internal activities were restrained from becoming ends in themselves by the theological and societal vision that informed them: a vision that has always kept the final goal of racial justice separate from the more proximate goals of independence and freedom (i.e., racial self-development). In short, blacks experienced freedom and independence in their churches, but the ultimate goal of racial justice necessitated societal reform in the larger white community. Racial self-development, religiously and morally under the principles of freedom and independence, was viewed by the black churches as a means to racial justice in the larger society. Thus while racism had forced the black churches into separate racial existence, and while their resistance to racism led them to make that separate existence a model of the good and the just, neither they nor their white foes ever intended that black separate development should approximate self-sufficiency. Any such attainment of complete racial independence would have implied that blacks had forsaken their ideal societal vision and that whites had surrendered their historic domination of blacks. As we have seen, many forces on both sides militated against such an outcome. Hence we can see the further complexity of the issue by the way the movement related its short-range and final goals.

But the independence and freedom of the black churches became the occasion for another form of moral ambiguity. From the end of the Reconstruction period to the end of the first half of the twentieth century, the black denominations manifested a dual posture toward racial injustice. On the one hand, they advocated aggressive action in behalf of civil and political rights while, on the other, they advocated a certain adjustment to the discriminatory laws, customs, and practices. They were able to do the latter without sacrificing their integrity, because they kept in mind that neither law nor any other force could cause them to believe that they were inferior or that racial injustice was justifiable. The rationale for the adjustment was based on a number of other grounds as well, all of which were stated in President E. C. Morris's presidential address to the National Baptist Convention in 1907: (1) that the laws of racial segregation had been due to the rapid progress that blacks had made since slavery in all dimensions of their life, progress that whites considered threatening; (2) that eventually the laws of racial discrimination and segregation would be repealed by future statesmen and by the Supreme Court; (3) that the good and respectable people would eventually see the worth of blacks and work vigorously for their full citizenship rights; (4) that whites would eventually see that the social separation[3] of the races could be maintained by granting to blacks civil and political rights; (5) that whites would eventually see and praise the patriotism of blacks.[4] The dual posture of the churches revealed a deeply rooted dilemma in their tradition, the horns of which were set forth clearly in the respective thought and action of W. E. B. DuBois and Booker T. Washington.

THE LACK OF POLITICAL WISDOM

Most scholars have observed that the black churches often unwittingly fell prey to the temptation of collapsing the larger society into its own surrogate world, thus denying the nature of the real world against which they were destined to struggle and on which they were dependent in so many ways. That temptation became evident each time the Baptist conventions and Methodist conferences elected their respective presidents and bishops, occasions that always bore striking similarities to election campaigns for the U.S. presidency — campaigning, demonstrations, smear tactics, concession speeches, victory parties, and the like. In his celebrated *Negro Baptist History U.S.A., 1750–1930,* L. G. Jordan described the election of the tenth president of the National Baptist Convention (St. Louis, 1922) as one of the three most eventful days in the then fifty years of the Convention's history.

Dr. Morris had served as president from September 1895 till his death, September 5, 1922. Who should succeed him, was the question to be settled in St. Louis. The candidates as announced were: Wesley G. Parks, D.D., LL.D., Philadelphia, Pa., who had by the death of Dr. Morris become president; Peter James Bryant, D.D., of Atlanta, Ga.; William H. Moses, D.D., of New York City; Moses W. D. Norman, D.D., LL.D., of Washington, D.C.; and Lacey K. Williams, D.D., of Chicago, Ill. For more than two months, the campaign was carried on. Much bitter feelings developed as it raged; the ugliest things ever said by one preacher about another were said by some of these brethren against their opponents.

Finally, the day for the meeting came and large delegations gathered in St. Louis from every part of the country. The enrollment showed 1800 delegates present. The several camps organized their forces on Tuesday and worked from Wednesday at 10:00 a.m., on through Thursday, all day, the second day for the election of officers, remaining in session until after 11 o'clock Thursday night. The hall was very cold and though we were without food or rest the voting went on, hour by hour. Finally the list of candidates narrowed down until it was Dr. Parks and Dr. Williams. No man living wishes to ever again go through such a nerve-racking siege. At 10:45 p.m., the tellers announced L. K. Williams' election. Ten years, or even five years earlier, the National Baptist Convention could not have stood such a strain, it would have split from the affects of such a controversy, but our men had grown wiser. In addition to this, there was no Bible or denominational principle involved in the case, so men shook hands and like all good Baptists should do, accepted the majority rule decision and all was well. Before the session was over, all previous bitterness gave place to a brotherly business session, which lasted during the remaining four days.[5]

Obviously, the election of leaders in the conventions and conferences of the black churches was and continues to be extremely important to all concerned. From within the churches no higher honor can befall a black minister than being elected to preside over the affairs of the denomination. Hence it is not difficult to see how easy it must have been for them to give certain internal denominational matters higher priority over other issues, including that of racial injustice. That is not to say, however, that the churches ever lost sight of racial injustice in any complete way. On the contrary, they have been foremost in the indomitable tasks of keeping the subject alive and in shaping the consciousness of their people concerning its meaning. But their failure to make injustice the subject of sustained and concerted deliberative activity has hindered the original political goal of transforming the wider society in the interest of racial justice. In other words, that failure has ensured an ad hoc status to all such political activities.

A careful analysis of the thought and action of the black churches inevitably leads to the proposition that their deliberative activities concerning effective opposition to racism has not been commensurate with their high consciousness of the problem. That is to say, they have not been sufficiently deliberative in their aim to effect racial justice in the wider society. In that respect, they have manifested few of the marks of political realism[6] typified in the tradition of American politics. Such a judgment is not intended to imply that they have been either apolitical or nonpolitical. Rather, we contend that political realism has not been institutionalized in the denominations in a way that does full justice to their mission. As agents of social change, they have failed to reach their mark not solely because of some stronger force of opposition acting on them, but because of a distinct lack of discernment on their part concerning the importance of constructive analytical and critical thought with respect to political purpose, effective strategy, and realizable goals. We do not mean to imply, however, any causal relationship between this political defect in the black denominations and the lack of racial justice in the larger society. Neither do we make this judgment for any futile purpose of attempting to correct the errors of the past, but rather to indicate that good political thought and action necessitate the concentrated efforts of many people thinking and acting cooperatively and constructively in a sustained manner.

Political realism has been called the art of the possible. It depicts a process of calculating effective means to realizable goals. Its orientation to consequences links it with the pragmatist tradition in American politics. Its basic moral weakness is the lack of fixed criteria for determining the quality of those consequences. Political idealism, on the other hand, has often been associated with utopianism. It portrays and promotes a final goal for society that is characterized by perfect harmony, a goal that is not a matter of deliberation. Its chief moral weakness lies in its apparent incapacity for historical realization. The tendency of political realists toward relativism and of political idealists toward fanaticism illustrates the nature of the conflict between them. In our judgment, political wisdom implies both, that is, a vision of the ideal society that regulates realizable goals commensurate with that vision. The lack of either an ideal vision or attainable goals implies a deficiency in political wisdom. Since the black churches embodied the one (the ideal societal vision) and not the other (deliberate choice of commensurable goals), we conclude that they have been lacking in political wisdom.

Since there is likely to be a correlation between the theological and the political thought of any group, the lack of creativity in the one is likely to reflect a similar lack in the other. Although the denominations have provided a forum for many of the most powerful, imaginative, and creative public leaders of the race (including educators, scholars, civil rights activists, legislators, and business persons), and although they have not restrained their local preachers from thinking and acting as they pleased in their respective situations, they have been reluctant nevertheless to draw significantly upon those resources in efforts to shape denominational policy on social issues. Further, they have been reluctant to set aside sufficient amounts of money as expressions of their institutional commitment to that part of their mission. Such a deliberate policy might have also influenced the work of the publishing houses and perhaps enabled them to break their longtime dependency on their white counterparts — a dependency that has been evidenced in both the structure and the content of most of their publications.[7] In their mission of social reform, the publishing facilities of the black churches have constituted an immense potential (although underutilized) resource.

Not infrequently, however, powerful thinkers have emerged in leadership positions in the denominations who, with diligence and vigor, have tried to persuade the churches to use their collective strength for the attainment of specific ecclesiastical and political goals. But the overall effect of these efforts has been miniscule. A good example is the assumed interest of African Methodism in church union. Almost from the beginning of their history both the A.M.E. Church and the A.M.E. Zion Church had recognized the importance of uniting themselves into one organic body, and to that end countless discussions have taken place.[8] Similarly, the goal of church union has been the substance of all the fraternal greetings delivered at the respective annual and quadrennial conferences for over a century. More sermons have been preached and more prayers offered on that subject than anyone could possibly know. Yet the goal was never realized, although seemingly unencumbered by either theological or ideological differences and apparently much desired by both groups. Hence one can only conclude that a primary reason must have been a lack of genuine commitment to the goal on the part of the denominations. In other words, the goal never became a major priority in the life of these denominations. Its symbolic and rhetorical value never became a political reality, the significance of which was argued well in the pleadings of Bishop Reverdy C. Ransom in 1939 when he reiterated the typical sentiment of his denomination on the matter.

Eight years ago, there was much talk on all sides of the union of the three great bodies of Negro Methodists. It has now become almost a dead issue. Will this General Conference revive it and pursue it until it becomes an accomplished fact? Where we are weak, all of us together might be strong. It is more, then, than an ecclesiastical and/or religious question. It lies at the very roots of the economic, political, and social welfare of the millions of our people. If we cannot achieve denominational union, the day of united action along business, commercial, civic, and political lines seems far distant.[9]

Since the reasons for the failure to realize church union among black Methodists cannot be attributable to racism, the causes must lie within the denominations themselves. We contend that not only the lack of political wisdom has been a serious constraint on the capacity of the black denominations to unite themselves organically into one church but also the lack of strong alliances among themselves and between black and white denominations — alliances for meaningful cooperative action aimed at social transformation in race relations. As a result the churches have made only indirect contributions to the development of wider publics either within the black community or between the races. We will return to this point later.

As we have already stated, it is virtually taken for granted among political realists that much effort must be devoted to strategizing, that is, to calculating effective means to desired goals. It is not strange, therefore, that very little strategizing has been done by the black denominations in relation to racial justice in the larger society. Although the black denominations have regularly appointed committees to report on the state of the nation, and in spite of the fact that each of the boards has offered its own respective analysis of the race problem in voluminous reports, the denominations have never instituted boards or departments on racial justice. Given the narrow and broad purposes of the black church independence movement, it is difficult to understand why the denominations chose not to have some structural provision for the systematic monitoring and critical analysis of the plight of blacks in the nation and, over a period of time, build up a depository of accumulated knowledge and concerted effort. The regular dissemination of information, allocation of monies, formation of alliances, development of programs, and the like, could have been the means of institutionalizing a deliberate style of thought and action aimed at societal transformation. But instead the churches came to rely heavily on the imaginative analyses and creative rhetoric of individual gifted orators as the means of keeping the people informed about the gravity of the problem. And that pattern has constituted a ritualistic tradition at both the Baptist conventions and the Methodist conferences. In addition to its appearance in the respective annual and quadrennial addresses of the Baptist presidents and Methodist bishops, as well as in the reports of the boards and the more focused report of the Committee on the State of the Nation, certain selected preachers and invited black leaders at each meeting were expected to deal with the race problem in some novel way and to affirm the race's convictions, inspire its spirit, applaud its past achievements, and stimulate its present efforts. Although many of those presentations are worthy of inclusion in the annals of the world's great orations, most failed to become important political treatises because little or no provision was made for their dissemination and utilization. Hence their effectiveness lasted only as long as that of any great speech that is dependent solely on the memory of its hearers. In short, these presentations were destined to have a short-lived effect. Thus countless sermons and speeches that could have become significant political and social documents, in addition to their religious content, have been lost because no agency sought to cause them to endure. The churches thereby decreased their effectiveness by relying too heavily on the oral tradition to the virtual exclusion of the written word and its preservation. Reliance on the oral traditions implies a fixed and stable world where order and continuity are dominant expectations. Critical, constructive thought, on the other hand, implies change, novelty, and growth. Hence the vision and style as well as the thought and action of the black churches have tended to be ritualistic, uncritically reflecting their respective traditions, and void of novel efforts toward change. They have been more retrospective than prospective, more priestly than prophetic, more conservative than novel.

It should be noted that since sermons comprised the primary form for most of these analyses, the people have been led generally to focus their attention on God's work as manifested in his kingdom rather than on what they themselves could do to bring about social change. The neglect of the latter implied that the experience of freedom and independence was limited to the confines of the black churches. A further inference was that the people must rely on the virtues of patience and goodwill in the face of persistent racial oppression. The black churches' countless condemnations of racist attitudes and practices in the larger society kept the race consciously aware of the problem. As already stated, that has constituted one of the major contributions that the churches have made to the political question. Although the imaginative and persuasive rhetoric of the preachers customarily discussed the problem at a high level of generality, individual persons of practical wisdom like Bishop Reverdy C. Ransom knew the importance of moving from generalizations to specific action.

> Shall the exploiters and oppressors of our people be challenged here by our united voice? We want work, we want bread, we desire to occupy our proper place in the body of politics. Shall we dedicate ourselves to fight on every front where the battle lines are drawn for freedom and opportunity, and against industrial exploitation? Shall we in the Presidential campaign this year, display enough intelligent political sagacity to take advantage of the main issue on which the two great parties are divided; namely, on the one hand that the policies of the New Deal violate the Constitution which should be upheld as handed down to us, and on the other that the Constitution should be liberalized by judicial interpretation, or otherwise in the interest of the present economic and social condition of the people of this country as a whole?
>
> Let those who would define the sacredness of the Constitution be faced with the fact that the Fifteenth Amendment is being flagrantly nullified and flouted. Let them be challenged to put a plank in their platform to come to the rescue of our voteless people in this country of American democracy.[10]

After quoting several texts from the prophetic tradition of the

Old Testament to refute those who might deny an integral relationship between religion and politics, Bishop Ransom summed up his theology in a way that has been familiar to many of his confreres both past and present.

> While Heaven is our final goal, our chief present concern is with life on this planet and human relations in our present society, to the end that the Kingdom of God may be established among men. I see little hope for the survival of the A.M.E. Church, or any other distinctly religious Negro denomination, if we do not so apply the Gospel of Christ as to make it a vital force in the life of society. While the National Association for the Advancement of Colored People and the Urban League may argue, petition, protest, and appeal, we are clothed with authority to declare, "Thus saith the Lord."[11]

The bishop then proceeded to admonish the church to become engaged deliberately and forthrightly in specific actions aimed at social justice.

> The world has little interest in us or concern about us as to what we do and what we say here. To them, we are just a group of Negroes here legislating and voting on matters that concern our Church. But once let us take up, in the name of a just and righteous God, the conditions that confront our people in this country; and the newspapers and every other public influence will immediately spring to attention. The sharecroppers of the South whose present conditions are but little removed from slavery are among the members of our Church who pay a large part of our Dollar Money from which our denomination derives its support. What have we done, what will we do, to help them to secure industrial and economic justice?[12]

Yet, in a way that has been typical of many church leaders, Bishop Ransom revealed a strong belief in the practical value of the church's use of religious authority to condemn racial injustice.

> The most flourishing domain of lynchers and mobs is found in communities that are the greatest devotees of religion and the Church. We should turn the searchlight of the Gospel of Jesus Christ upon them and keep it centered there. If he thought about it at all, Senator Borah knew he was running little risk of repudiation at the ballot box by the great bulk of Negro voters when he frankly stated that, if elected President, he would veto a Federal law against lynching. No political party would nominate him or any other man out

of sympathy with our people if it knew that every Negro pulpit in the country would thunder against him as from Heaven until its blast resounded throughout the nation.

While the weapons of our welfare are not carnal, we should make them mighty through God to the tearing down of the strongholds of the wicked.[13]

After praising the church for its independence of management and control, Bishop Ransom admonished the church to develop its own agenda and cease following the unworthy programs and practices of the white churches. Finally, before launching into a rhetorical flourish with respect to the eschatological hope, he set forth his doctrine of the church clearly in one sentence: "The Church that shall survive must know neither race, color, nor nationality nor recognize distinctions of wealth, class or station, but only the dignity and sacredness of our common humanity."[14] He went on to say that the church and its leaders must be prophetic, and in fact that a measure of their divine call should be their ability to proclaim the gospel in evil times:

The bishop and ministers that lead this Church must have their call and commission from God, and the genuineness of their credentials and the divine authority with which they are clothed must be witnessed by their power and faith to proclaim and uphold the Gospel message in an evil time. It must be a prophetic Church, not only beholding the Lord and lifting up, while the cherubim cry "Holy, Holy, Holy," round His throne; but while the Church is marching through the wilderness, they must point to the realm of hope and promise that lies just beyond. They must proclaim liberty to the captives — those that are socially, economically, and politically disinherited — with authority of a Divine justice that will not rest until every fetter of injustice and oppression is broken.[15]

We have quoted at length from Bishop Ransom's address because it typifies the dominant theological and political understandings held by the black churches in the nineteenth and twentieth centuries, understandings that have changed very little from one generation to the next. In fact, there is little difference in the reasoning between nineteenth- and twentieth-century black denominational leaders on theological and political issues. That reveals not only a basic conservatism in both thought and action, but it also portends a certain satisfaction with fixed and facile analyses of the race problem. Perhaps the latter is an inevitable consequence among those who view the world as divided by two forces: evil and good, that is, racism and its opposition. Ambiguous and complex perspectives necessarily threaten such a world. Like soldiers at war who are content with simple analyses concerning the issues at stake, black churches also have been satisfied with traditional understandings of the race problem which, for the most part, have been rooted in folk wisdom. That, in itself, is not a defect. Rather, it can be the strongest indicator of the problem's longevity. But when divorced from critical contemporary knowledge, it can appear antiquated to both the learned and the well-informed. Analogously, the symptoms of many diseases have remained the same from one generation to another, but none will deny that immense progress has been made in the nature of medical diagnosis and the concomitant prescriptions for cure. Similarly, in the social sphere there has been considerable advance in our understandings of the societal system and the way its many parts relate to each other as condition and possibility. Apart from occasional appearances at denominational conventions and conferences, no serious efforts have been made by the churches to conjoin their wisdom with the knowledge and skills of black scholars like W. E. B. DuBois, Kelly Miller, John Hope, Alain Locke, Charles H. Wesley, E. Franklin Frazier, to mention a few past greats. And that neglect has continued to the present day. Any presumption that black scholars as a group, then or now, would have shunned serious discussion with the churches is totally ungrounded. The absence of any firm alliance between the two has rendered each a disservice by a denial of the other's resources. Further, their separation has provided a vacuum that has often been filled by stereotypes of the one by the other. Regrettably, black scholars have been deprived of the value of association with a major institution in the black community, and the churches have been deprived of the constructive criticism of sociologists, political scientists, psychologists, economists, artists, and others on the pressing racial problem of the day.

THE BLACK CHURCHES' IMPLIED
SOCIOLOGY

A careful analysis of the thought of Bishop Ransom, quoted previously, and that of most black church leaders reveals a firm commitment to a common societal vision, namely, a society that acknowledges as significant neither race, color, nationality, class, nor station. Many have been unaware that their vision has been identical with the so-called melting pot theory that has been implicit in the American consciousness both as fact and norm throughout much of the twentieth century. It was formally put forward as a sociological theory in the 1950s as an explanation of the assimilation process that the European immigrants underwent in this country. A recent description of that process by one of its original progenitors, Nathan Glazer, demonstrates that identification.

> The ideal was one of full assimilation of all immigrant groups to a common cultural type, so that ethnicity would play no role in individual consciousness, groups would not be formed around ethnic interests, "hyphenated Americanism" would be a thing of the past, and the United States would be as homogeneous in its Americanness as the nations of the old world were in their Englishness, their Frenchness, their Germanness, their Italianness.[16]

Glazer goes on to say that the above value has functioned normatively for Americans for a very long while and, in his judgment, it should continue to do so because it offers a solution to the conflictual problems Americans will continue to face with the steady growth of ethnic pluralism. He is aware, however, of the limitations attending that solution.

> Leave aside the fact that the old Americans did not seem to hold this ideal in full consistency. They expected abandonment of difference, but would not make a payoff of full acceptance of those who had given up their difference. Leave aside the fact that even the nations of the old world have lost their homogeneity, to the extent they had it, under the impact of the economic changes of the past three decades. Leave aside the realism of expecting people to give up

ethnic attributes, attachments, and loyalties within any brief period
of time. This still is an ideal that is worth holding in mind and
presenting as probably the best outcome for America. Difference,
alas, almost always becomes a source of conflict. Assimilation has
already proceeded so far with some groups, specifically the European ethnic groups, that it is not an unreasonable hope.[17]

Glazer's position implies the goal of full cultural assimilation on
the part of ethnic groups, and that goal is best illustrated with
reference to those European immigrant groups that have become
fully assimilated into American culture. The major difference
between them and blacks, however, has been the racial factor.
Blacks have always known that they were not so fully assimilatable
short of widespread interracial mating—the latter, incidentally,
having been the greatest fear of white Americans and, ironically,
the least desired objective of black Americans.[18] While Glazer and
others have not dealt adequately with the serious constraint that
the racial factor presents to his theory of assimilation, neither have
the black churches critically assessed their own normative societal
vision in the light of their perceptions of the impact of race on that
vision.

Recently many sociologists, black and white, have abandoned
the melting-pot theory in favor of various theories of cultural
pluralism, thus setting the terms of the present debate. The
assimilationism implied by the melting-pot theory aims at a
homogeneous culture, the full realization of which is thought by
some to be impossible as long as a visible racial factor is present.
Theories of cultural pluralism, on the other hand, emphasize the
importance of inclusion while affirming various differences of
race, ethnicity, and religion. This position has been advocated by
the noted Talcott Parsons, who rejects both the assimilationist
theory and that of separation. The essence of his argument is contained in the following quotation:

> To identify non-discrimination (that is, inclusion) too strongly with
> complete "color-blindness" might be to throw away a very precious
> asset, not only for the Negro, but for American Society as a whole.
> My own view is that the healthiest line of development will be not
> only the preservation, but the actual building up, of the solidarity

of the Negro community and the sense that being a Negro has positive value. In the process there is the danger of cultivating
separatism, as most conspicuously exemplified by the Black Mus-
lims. But the pluralistic solution, which has been stressed throughout this discussion, is neither one of separation — with or without
equality — nor of assimilation, but one of full participation combined with the preservation of identity. The American Jewish and
Catholic groups have, by and large, been able to achieve this goal.[19]

Political order is obviously less difficult to maintain in a
homogeneous society than in a pluralistic one, and that fact has
often conditioned the preferences of the majority group. Further,
empirical judgments about whether or not America is homogeneous or pluralistic have often been quickly translated into normative judgments. Social scientists on either side of this debate have
been enormously influential in shaping social policy for the past
several decades. The black denominations have not related themselves self-consciously to that debate. Although their ideal societal
vision appears to be assimilationist, their strong commitment to
the future continuation of black schools, colleges, and churches
necessarily draws upon the arguments of cultural pluralists. Hence
they would serve themselves well by a greater knowledgeability
about the theories, findings, and implications of social scientific
analyses. In fact, there is no other way of developing accurate
knowledge about how trends in the political, legal, cultural,
social, economic systems impact on the problem of racial justice.
We admit that analyses by church leaders at the turn of the century were not only simplistic but quite accurate, because at that
time 90 percent of blacks lived in rural southern areas characterized by universal racial segregation and discrimination. Yet even
then those analyses were not fully adequate for understanding the
situation of northern urban blacks, and less so after the massive
migrations of blacks to urban areas during and following World
War I. Finally, the demise of the Jim Crow system in the 1960s
necessitates in our time more adequate ways of understanding the
nature of the problem and especially the impact of urbanism in its
present form and function. Some have contended that unlike the
European immigrant groups the race problem has become, in the
mid-twentieth century, an urban class problem.[20] There are a

growing number of black scholars on the scene today who argue similarly, namely, that racism exists, but it alone does not explain the condition in which blacks find themselves because of the impact of political, legal, and economic changes on race relations. The dominant tendency of the black churches has been to dismiss such arguments as ideological "sellouts" instead of trying to understand them and, when possible, making a rational rebuttal to them. We tentatively conclude that because of their separation from the social scientists, the black churches have been working with very limited understandings of the nature of the race problem — understandings that are likely to be outdated because of the changes that have taken place in the nation and the impact of those changes on the significance of racism. Adequacy in understanding the nature of the problem in its contemporary form is a necessary condition for political wisdom.

THE BLACK CHURCHES AND
THEIR ALLIANCES

Although the organizational and financial structure of the black denominations does not reflect any major commitment to sociopolitical reform, and despite the fact that the churches have not effectively utilized the various resources available to them, they nevertheless have given significant leadership, moral support, financial assistance, and the use of their physical facilities to a large number of organizations in the black community dedicated to the struggle against racism. In many instances these particular organizations either had been founded by the black churches or had been in close association with them. By encouraging them to be autonomous and self-supporting, the churches have been able to give their support to a variety of different types of organizations, exhibiting alternative styles of leadership and purpose while not becoming predominantly identified with any particular one. Consequently they have been able to give their official blessing to such varied organizations as the following: the National Afro-American League and its successor, the National Afro-American Council; the Niagara Movement and its successor, the National Association for the Advancement of Colored People (NAACP); the

National Equal Rights League, started by William Monroe Trotter as an alternative to the white supported NAACP; the National Urban League, which grew out of the combined efforts of the Committee on Urban Conditions Among Negroes in New York City and the National League for the Protection of Colored Women, both of which had had the support of the black churches; the Congress of Racial Equality; the Southern Christian Leadership Conference; Operation Breadbasket (later called People United to Save Humanity — PUSH); Opportunities Industrialization Center. A close analysis of the above organizations reveals that all of them share the common ideal societal vision and similar methods of protest and negotiation for full participation of blacks in all areas of public life. Further, those organizations that the churches have tended to support have almost always been interracial in membership, a fact that reveals more clearly than anything else their commitment to the ideal societal vision. Conversely, no organization that has rejected that societal vision has ever received the official support of the black churches, for example, the Nation of Islam, the United Negro Improvement Association of Marcus Garvey, the Revolutionary Action Movement, the National Negro Congress of the 1930s, to mention only a few. Similarly, the black churches have been reluctant to express any strong support for such cultural and literary movements as Black Power or the Harlem Renaissance, partly because of the strong positive valuation each gave to the race factor. The churches have been suspicious of any type of racial chauvinism, considering it romantic at best and racist at worse.

This discussion would be incomplete were we not to reiterate the important communicative role the black church publishing houses have played in the racial struggle. For many decades prior to the rise of the black secular press, the black church papers served as major protest instruments against racism through the dissemination of information, the interpretation of events affecting the race's welfare, and advocacy for specific forms of resistance.

Thus the deficiency of the churches in practical wisdom in no way implies a lack of important contributions they have made directly and indirectly to the political dimensions of the struggle for racial justice. Rather, our clarification of the problems that have attended their efforts defines the limits of those contributions and, it is hoped, challenges the contemporary churches to enhance their activities and power by utilizing all of the potential resources inherent in the race.

NOTES

1. This fact could be evidenced in a variety of ways, but for our purpose it is sufficient to demonstrate it by reference to the A.M.E. Social Creed read to the 1936 quadrennial conference by Bishop Reverdy Ransom. Apart from the articles on racial justice, a broad consensus existed between black and white churches on the others. See Appendix A.

2. Further, no small amount of energy was used in resolving the many conflicts that developed from time to time within the denominations and that often threatened institutional stability and unity. Not infrequently those conflicts had to be resolved in the civil courts, and on two occasions the National Baptist Convention was split as a result.

3. It is interesting to note that the black churches have never advocated full social equality of the races, i.e., unrestrained social mixing of the races.

4. *Journal of the 27th Annual Session of the National Baptist Convention held with the Metropolitan Baptist Church, Washington, D.C., September 11–16, 1907* (Nashville: National Baptist Publishing Board, 1908), 26ff.

5. L. G. Jordan, *Negro Baptist History U.S.A., 1750–1930* (Nashville: Sunday School Publishing Board, 1930), 142–43.

6. It is important to note that we are aware of those who argue to the contrary by attempting to prove that the political realism of the black churches has been seen in their instinct for self-preservation. They argue that the churches self-consciously chose to maintain a low institutional profile in political activity in order to be a foil in the movement for racial justice and to deflect elsewhere attacks that might have been aimed at them. In his defense of the apparent conservatism of the black churches, Carter G. Woodson stated the following: "Acting as a conservative force among Negroes, the Church has been a sort of balance wheel. It has not been unprogressive but rather wise in its generation in not rushing forward to a radical position in advance of public opinion. In other words, the Negro church has known how far it can safely instruct its people to go in righting their own wrongs, and this conservatism has no doubt saved the Negro from the fate of other oppressed groups who have suffered extermination because of the failure to handle their case more diplomati-

cally" (Carter G. Woodson, *The History of the Negro Church* [Washington, D.C.: Associated Publishers, 1921], 278–79). While we respect the reasoning involved in explaining the caution exercised by the black churches in their political activity, it is our judgment, nevertheless, that political idealism has dominated their political thought and action at the expense of political realism.

7. This point is supported by Kelly Miller Smith in a recent essay, "Religion as a Force in Black America," in *The State of Black America 1982*, edited by James D. Williams (New Brunswick, N.J.: Transaction Books, 1982), 229ff.

8. These two denominations have been carrying on similar discussions with the Christian Methodist Episcopal Church since its independence in 1875, and the A.M.E. Zion Church has been in conversation with the Methodist Episcopal Church for reunion since the Civil War.

9. George A. Singleton, *The Romance of African Methodism* (New York: Exposition Press, 1952), 150–51.

10. Ibid., 151–52.

11. Ibid., 152.

12. Ibid., 152–53.

13. Ibid., 153.

14. Ibid., 154.

15. Ibid., 154–55.

16. Nathan Glazer, "Politics of a Multiethnic Society," in *Ethnic Relations in America*, edited by Lance Liebman (New York: Prentice-Hall, 1982), 148.

17. Ibid., 148–49.

18. This fact was established by Gunnar Myrdal's study *An American Dilemma*, 2 vols. (New York: Harper & Brothers, 1944).

19. Talcott Parsons, "Full Citizenship for the Negro American?" in *The Negro American*, edited by Talcott Parsons and Kenneth B. Clark (Cambridge, Mass.: Houghton Mifflin Co., 1966), 750.

20. This view has been offered by Talcott Parsons in his essay "Full Citizenship for the Negro American?" in *The Negro American*, edited by Parsons and Clark, 73ff. The most recent proponent of this position is a prominent black scholar, William Julius Wilson, who argues that race is no longer the dominant factor in understanding the economic plight of blacks, but, rather, that class constitutes the nature of black subordination because of the impact of industrialism on race relations. See especially his book *The Declining Significance of Race: Blacks and Changing American Institutions* (Chicago: University of Chicago Press, 1978).

5

Embodiments of Communal Power

INDEPENDENCE AS THE CONDITION
FOR FREEDOM

In his 1946 address before the Extra Session of the African Methodist Episcopal Church Conference, Bishop Ransom depicted a parallel development between the history of the black churches and the nation. The significance of his insight cannot be overemphasized, because it virtually linked the institutionalization of racial separation with the genesis of the republic. His viewpoint also implied a denial of the claim advanced by many that substantial improvement in race relations had followed the Revolutionary War, which had nurtured in all the spirit of liberty, independence, and freedom.

> The second thing I want to say is that we appreciate our relation to our nation's formation and growth. I mean the parallel history of the African Methodist Episcopal Church, and the United States of America. In 1787, when the Constitution was being framed in Philadelphia, we were five or six blocks away on sixth and Lombard, organizing the African Methodist Episcopal Church. As the first lines of the bill proclaiming independence for the United Colonies from Great Britain were struck off, we too, floated our flag six blocks away for manhood, and independence to the establishment of a Church to the glory of God.[1]

A similar statement could have been made by the black Baptists as well, since their first pioneer churches were founded in Georgia and South Carolina a few years prior to the Constitutional Convention.[2] Similarly, less than a decade later, the African Methodist Episcopal Zion Church in New York City had taken its first stride toward independence. Collectively, these groups symbolized the universal thrust of blacks for racial separation in order to effect self-expression.

We contend that some measure of independence has always been a necessary condition for black self-expression. Hence the black church independence movement provided for blacks what the Declaration of Independence provided for the nation, namely, the condition for freedom and self-actualization. We also contend that even during slavery, slaves had some form of independent space (permissible or not), otherwise they would never have been able to place their unique mark on the Christian faith. Since the dates, places, and authorship of the so-called Negro Spirituals are unknown, E. Franklin Frazier described their locus as "the invisible institution," an apt portrayal of the underground rendezvous that characterized slave religion.

> Our preachers were usually plantation folks just like the rest of us. Some man who had a little education and had been taught something about the bible would be our preacher. The coloured folks had their code of religion, not nearly so complicated as the white man's religion, but more closely observed. . . . When we had our meetings of this kind, we held them in our own way and were not interfered with by the white folks.[3]

Only in their independent space could the essential structures of black religion appear, chief among which has been the feature of black leadership over a black constituency. Albert Raboteau gives paramount importance to this notion of independence when he writes that "at the core of the slave's religion was a private place, represented by the cabin room, the overturned pot, the prayin' ground, and the 'hush harbor.'" This place the slave kept as his own. No matter how religious the master might be, the slave knew that the master's religion did not countenance prayers for his slaves' "freedom in this world."[4] Only under conditions of racial separation have blacks been able to act in their own way, that is, to assess their own needs, shape their own agenda, determine their own priorities, develop their own styles of acting. Mays and

Nicholson concluded several decades ago that the attributes of
black church ownership and control constituted the institution's
primary *genius*.[5] Only in that separate religious space that we call
the black church has the race found adequate independence from
the larger white hostile world not only to experience temporary
relief from the impact of racism but also to initiate, design, and
implement methods of adjustment and of resistance to that inimi-
cal force. Only in such a space has the church been able to develop,
enhance, and nurture the moral and social life of the race which,
as we have seen, has always been viewed by blacks as a necessary
but not a sufficient goal — rather, a precondition for external relationships with the larger society.

The experience of self-governance provided blacks with the
opportunity to practice the basic rights of citizenship long before
the basic rights became constitutionally guaranteed and politically
enacted for them. Ironically, it became the destiny of the black
preachers to emerge as the freest of all persons, black and white
alike, because they embodied the condition of independence and
freedom more than any other. In their pulpits they could condemn
virtually any social evil in either the white or the black community
without fearing the possibility of censureship. Their condemnations of the established powers of the larger society for aiding and
abetting racial injustice ensured the jubilant praise of their constituents and never their reproach. Only some willful violation of the
black community's trust ever threatened their prestige and position. Accordingly, both they and their people exercised considerable power in relation to one another and together in relation to
the white society.

The independence of the black churches has provided blacks
with the necessary condition for the experience of freedom, which
has had the following visible characteristics: (1) black men in positions of authority and power, shaping the values, perspectives,
aspirations, and activities of the black masses both in their separate racial existence and in their relationships with the white
world; (2) indigenous styles of worship, music, song, prayers, and
preaching intended to inspire the soul of the race to express its
deepest needs, hopes, and dreams; (3) an internal church organi-

zational structure reflective of its mission to exemplify the parent-hood of God and the kinship of all peoples by proclaiming in word and deed the equality of the races; (4) ecclesiastical programs expressing high priority for the educational, moral, and social development of the race along with various forms of advocacy for racial justice and equality; (5) a black democratic constituency exhibiting great pride in its church tradition and exercising its vote with extreme care when electing its ruling officers; (6) a physical edifice symbolizing racial solidarity and religious meaning; (7) a widely known support system for all other black organizations and institutions (including many black businesses) committed to serv-ing the welfare of the race. Further, even a casual survey of the black community would reveal widespread public support for the potentialities and the benevolences of the black churches. Most important, the black churches view themselves and their distinc-tive characteristics as vivid contrasts to both the form and the sub-stance of the white churches. Consequently, they have been paradigmatic for the organized life of the black community, because they actualize among themselves the condition of inde-pendence and the experience of freedom more adequately than any other organized effort.

THE NATURE OF POWER IN
THE BLACK CHURCHES

Independent black churches have always been in conflict with the larger white society, a conflict that has often resulted in con-siderable ambivalence among blacks toward Christianity per se. On the one hand, blacks have loved and affirmed Jesus, while, on the other, they have rejected "white Christianity." The latter dispo-sition has usually been radicalized in the ideologies of so-called black nationalist groups. During the first century of their enslave-ment, blacks refused to accept Christianity, because they associated it wholly with the religion of their masters — a religion that viewed them as slaves by nature. Only after they had had the opportunity to reform the religion of their overseers did they accept Christianity. Hence the fundamental principle that we call the black Christian tradition was a necessary condition for the Christianization of the race.[6] In other words, independence and Christian reform logically preceded the religious conversion of black Americans.

But the mission of the black churches has always transcended their own constituency by aiming at the reform of the larger white society, that is, causing the latter to practice racial justice as an expression of genuine Christian understanding and devotion. Their mission, therefore, has had both an internal and an external dimension in that they have sought religious, moral, and political reform in both the black and the white community, though not in the same respect.

It is, however, ironic that the primary instruments of social reform employed by the black churches have been the religious and political ideals of their white oppressors, namely, (1) the biblical idea of the parenthood of God and the kinship of all people and (2) the constitutional idea that all people are created equal and endowed by their Creator with certain unalienable rights. The religious idea has been used by blacks as a means of redeeming both the ecclesiastical and the civil religions of the nation, while the political idea has constituted the grounds of justification for their claims of racial justice. Blacks have derived similar moral obligations from both ideas. Consequently, they have rightly viewed both as integrally related — indeed, the political as derivative from the religious, since the religious is more universal.

The churches' use of the above instruments of social reform implied a commitment to wage the struggle for racial justice within the nation rather than from without either by migration or revolution. Further, their belief in biblical anthropology and its assumed affirmation by the Constitution implied devotion to non-violent legitimate means of advocacy. Neither violence nor colonization ever gained domicile in the black churches, even though a number of its members and a few disgruntled leaders from time to time opted for such strategies.

The existence of the black churches has always implied an indictment against the racial values of white America's religious, political, and social institutions. Since the black churches have the ear and support of the black masses more than any other institution, the black churches have constituted a place of power both within the black community and as the black community's representative in the white society. Their position of institutional primacy in the black community has enabled them to be the locus of racial social solidarity which, in turn, has comprised the basis of all cooperative activity aimed at racial advance. In fact, their historical function of maintaining and enhancing racial solidarity gained for them the right to speak on behalf of the race whenever they wished. Consequently, they have been the major lobbying force of the black community for racial justice which, in their judgment, has always meant racial equality.[7]

Further, the capacity of the black churches to establish and maintain racial solidarity reveals both the religious and the political basis of their power. Religiously, they have provided the community with that common set of fundamental ideas, rituals, symbols, and beliefs which unites the race in spite of its many differences. Politically, their power is understood in part as a persuasive capacity to achieve a moral effect within both the black and the white community. It is important to note that this form of power has often been viewed as more effective in the long run than varying forms of coercive power, a view that has been succinctly stated by Martin E. Marty:

> People may not always believe what their official church bodies wish them to or claim that they do. But it is shared belief, prayer, and experience that mold power, not — in voluntary groups like religions are — the ability to raise armies or taxes or the ability to ostracize or shun effectively.[8]

Although their success in the white community has been disturbingly slow, the black churches have been very effective in creating a massive consensus in the black community concerning the rightness of their quest for racial equality, which alone has constituted the substance of their solidarity. Yet we do not intend to imply that their reform efforts in the larger society have been insignificant. On the contrary, their various forms of initiative and support have had both influence and impact on the body politic.

These include such momentous events as the underground railroad, the abolition movement, the anti-colonization movement, and the civil rights movement. Further, the black churches have been at the forefront of all those crises in race relations that have split the white churches and the nation into two opposing sides — for example, the antebellum regional split in the Methodist, Presbyterian, and Baptist denominations; the Civil War; Reconstruction; Jim Crowism. Interestingly, these major national events in the racial struggle were also in tandem with other forms of interregional conflict.[9]

In their self-understanding, blacks have viewed themselves as a powerless race with considerable capacity for expressing love and justice. In our view, such a self-understanding is contradictory, because it implies that one can act in love and justice apart from power. We hold, on the contrary, that in the order of nature, power precedes love and justice because it is coterminous with life itself. In other words, to be alive is to express the capacity *to be*, and that is an expression of power. To view oneself as powerless is always self-destructive, because it contributes to the formation of a disposition of inferiority which leads to low self-esteem, both individually and collectively, and in turn dissipates motivation. But the capacity to unite power with justice and love is the distinctive function of human beings.

Power is the capacity both to produce an effect and to undergo an effect.[10] Like many in the society at large, the black churches have tended to understand power as the ability to produce an effect. Consequently, they have tended to view whites as having paramount power evidenced in their ability to have maintained the slave system for over three centuries and racial subjugation for another one hundred years. Correspondingly, they have viewed themselves as powerless because they have not been able to produce their desired effect on the white community in any full and complete way. That is to say, their inability to dominate whites as the whites have dominated them has led both blacks and whites to conclude that blacks are powerless. Since the attainment of that kind of power — namely, the ability to manipulate, shape, and control others — requires similar means of coercion, and since neither the black churches nor the black community at large has ever committed themselves fully to such methods, it is not difficult to see why they have failed to gain such power. Further, the structure of oppression is such that the oppressed are never able to possess the kind of power their oppressors have, short of the successful use of violence (or the threat of such), deliberately employed in its pursuit. Although the black churches and other select organizations and persons have been able to wield some measure of control in the black community, they have never been able to do so in the white community. Sometimes, however, strategic coalitions with sympathetic whites have been effective in gradually producing limited effects on the body politic, effects, incidentally, that have issued in most of the significant milestones reached in the long pilgrimage toward racial justice. Unfortunately, however, the coalitions themselves have been fragile and tenuous, because their internal relationships have tended to be dominated by this controlling type of power which always works in opposition to mutuality, trust, and cooperation. Such an orientation to power has also been a primary cause of the many and varied conflicts that have permeated the internal life of the black churches as well as their relationships with one another.

Bernard Loomer rightly calls this type of power "unilateral power," because it is interested only in its own purposes and tends always to reduce the other to a means to its own ends. Consequently, it is unable to exhibit concern for the other's total being. Its activities inevitably contribute to the emotional estrangement from those to whom it is related. Hence it destroys love and is incapable of doing justice.

It is obvious that the historical conflict that has existed between the black churches and the larger white society has not resulted in any profound existential estrangement from whites by blacks. In spite of the persistent involvement of blacks in their advocacy for racial justice and their opposition to racism, as protagonists they have rarely defined white antagonists solely as enemy. Although they have viewed the Ku Klux Klan as wholly hostile, the race has refrained from viewing all white Americans similarly. Unlike a typical military battle in which the enemy is considered unredeemable and fully deserving of death, blacks responded to the KKK mainly by avoidance and rarely resorted to violence even in self-defense. Martin Luther King, Jr., rightly captured the spirit of the black community when he said repeatedly that nonviolent resistance is redemptive. While its active dimension fails to compromise evil, its passive side manifests an alternative method of response that keeps the conditions of communication open rather than closed. The availability of such conditions implies the redeemability of the opponent. Let us hasten to add, however, that even short of violence, certain types of withdrawal from the situation can also imply a complete loss of confidence in the other's moral capacity for change. That has usually been the disposition of various black nationalist groups toward whites.

The predominant way in which blacks have responded to their hostile environment evidences a form of power that is quite different from unilateral power. It has been called by many names in the tradition, such as "soul force," "moral suasion," "moderation," "nonviolence." But all the names are suggestive of an active openness toward the other, and that constitutes the distinctive quality of this type of power. It is what Bishop William J. Walls was attempting to describe in the following:

> The story of the struggle of the black race to achieve full citizenship is the story of the African Methodist Episcopal Zion church. Through the years, we tenaciously held back the bitterness and preached the gospel of nonviolence. The prayers, faith, tears, bloodshed, loss of life, organizing, mass meetings, negotiating, sit-ins, arrests, marches, fund-raising, rallies, tortures, warfares, freedom-rides, defeats, disappointments, harassments, threats, and victories, bespeak the total involvement and desire to practice our love, love which "worketh no ill to his neighbor: therefore love is the fulfilling of the law."[11]

It is what Bernard Loomer called "relational power" and what Paul Tillich called the "power of being." We choose to call it "communal power" because of its implicit drive for unity between the contending parties. Communal power is a force that recognizes the potentiality for community and strives unceasingly for its realization. While it is profoundly concerned about the welfare of the other, it is primarily concerned about maintaining the capacity for a continued viable relationship. Preserving that capacity has been of paramount importance to the black churches in their struggle for racial justice. Their recognition of the nation's racism has been for them what a diagnosis is for a physician. That is to say, they have been bent on curing the disease without destroying the patient. Further, their methods have been respectful of the larger organism, its laws, values, and functions. Moreover, they have refrained from viewing the disease as terminal and hence have not withdrawn curative activities. In fact, they have maintained their faith in the proposition that the problem would one day be resolved.

It is the essence of communal power to sustain the potentiality for communal relationship regardless of the circumstances. Consequently, it never contemplates retaliation or revenge. Rather, it endlessly seeks more effective means of fostering communal experience. The black churches as well as many other organizations in the black community have held firmly to their love for America's potentiality for interracial community and have refused to compromise that love by acts of vengeance. Further, it must be said that their love for America should not be construed to mean a pathological love for whites at the expense of self-affirmation, but rather a love for whites and blacks living harmoniously in community which, in their view, constitutes what America ought to be.

The many severe diatribes against America frequently delivered by stalwart leaders of the black community and its churches have been basic expressions of frustration, disgust, disappointment, disillusionment, and even hatred of the nation's actual racist practices. But their harsh criticisms have been rooted in a fundamental belief in America's potentiality for good, namely, for interracial justice. Viewed out of their context, various speeches by such unwavering patriots as Frederick Douglass, Henry McNeil Turner, Reverdy C. Ransom, E. C. Morris, Adam Clayton Powell, Jr., Martin Luther King, Jr., and others, would seem to be the flaming denunciations of thoroughgoing revolutionaries. Instead, their rhetoric has served to express the wrath of the race's prophets deeply loyal to the biblical view of humanity which, they were convinced, had been affirmed by the nation's founding fathers. Hence their total identification with the goal they sought, and their firm belief in the nation's potentiality to embody it caused them, from time to time, to pour forth eloquent criticism not only as a means of expressing their own emotions but also as a possible way of arousing the sensitivities of whites and to prick their consciences.

In their struggle against racism, black churches have never understood themselves as a narrow self-interest group seeking only their own satisfaction. On the contrary, they have sought to save the republic from self-destruction and to redeem its democracy by calling for the destruction of the malignant racism that threatens the well-being of the nation. Thus the good they have sought has been a new relationship between blacks and whites that would be characterized by equity, goodwill, and harmony.

It is not our intention to imply that the universe of black Americans has always expressed communal power. On the contrary, some have expounded unilateral power and in rhetoric and deed have turned either to violence or to colonization elsewhere. But the black churches have never been a part of either scheme in any official or public way. Those church persons who eventually adopted such an orientation either relinquished their association with the churches or formed new religious associations.[12]

The notion of communal power enables us to understand better the many perplexing puzzlements one encounters in undertaking a critical analysis of the black American experience. Throughout this inquiry we have found ourselves troubled by the seeming absence of bitterness, hostility, violence, and despair. In spite of conditions of slavery, lynching, terrorism, segregation, discrimination, and the social stamp of inferiority, the primary source materials within black America (religious and secular) are replete with expressions of patriotic zeal, interracial goodwill, respect for law and order, and devotion to America's potentiality for racial justice. Apart from a view of communal power, either we must conclude that black Americans for the most part accommodated themselves to racism and thereby contributed to their own degradation or we are driven to do revisionist history by selectively thematizing those events, speeches, and personalities that manifest militant aggression, underground radicalism, revolutionary ideologies, and violent uprisings.

We must make it unequivocally clear that communal power is not the opposite of unilateral power. That would be mere passivity or the total lack of any capacity whatsoever. Communal power, rather, is the capacity both to produce an effect and to undergo an effect. Hence it includes unilateral power but is not identical with it. Its chief weakness lies in its tendency to neglect that aspect of itself and become so completely focused on the reconciliation of the other that it falls prey to the danger of making the other's feelings, understandings, and activities normative for itself, lest its own needs and interests get in the way of the other and hinder the relationship. In doing so, it distorts the relationship both potentially and actually by failing to make its own claims on it. By doing so, it renders itself weak in the eyes of the other as well as in its own eyes. By giving the accent of primacy to the other it diminishes itself and thereby decreases the value of its own contribution to the relationship. Hence it tends to view itself as inferior, and that disposition contributes to the unilateral power of the other. Unwittingly, that tendency militates against community.

The black churches have been guilty of distorting communal power in this way. Their devotion to their ideal societal vision has made them vulnerable, in both speech and action, to the pursuit of goals that have been universal, abstract, and formal. C. Eric Lincoln argues that the decisive difference between the Montgomery bus boycott and the history of the black churches is that black religious leaders for the first time challenged the white establishment to a struggle over something specific and in which one side or the other had to emerge as victor.[13] The victory that blacks achieved in that event was unprecedented, and it changed the whole history of the black struggle for racial justice, to say nothing of its psychological impact on all who participated directly or indirectly. That type of activity enabled blacks to become initiators of action rather than mere respondents. In that event we see black religious leaders utilizing communal power in its full sense, that is, aiming at producing an effect and undergoing an effect, and both in the interest of enhancing community. In this respect the civil rights movement of Martin Luther King, Jr., was a precursor to the black power movement which initially in the eyes of many, including King himself, was viewed as the antithesis of communal power.

COMMUNAL POWER AND BLACK POWER

The story of the black power movement has been told by several writers, but none has understood it more astutely than Gayraud Wilmore in his interpretation of the relationship between black religion and black radicalism.[14] He understands black power to be a phenomenon that emerged at a period of profound crisis in the twentieth-century civil rights struggle — a time when black America had come perilously close to losing confidence in the American Dream and turning away from the optimism that had characterized much of their past activities. Disappointment, disillusionment, and anger motivated many blacks in the mid-1960s to assume a more hardheaded, realistic posture toward white America by becoming strong advocates of unilateral power for blacks as a corrective to the traditional concentration on moral suasion and its implied consensual basis.

> A new tough-minded skepticism, self-interest and sense of survival has slowly taken over Black America. . . .
> Black Power meant that only by Black people solidifying their ranks through a new consciousness of history and culture, building political and economic power, and being willing to legitimize ethnocentrism, group self-interest and even defensive violence, if necessary, could they hope to survive the onslaught of repression following in the wake of disillusioned white liberalism, and take control of their own future.[15]

The new deliberative style initiated by the black power movement clearly revealed its distinctive difference from that of the civil rights movement. Whereas the latter had always welcomed the participation of sympathetic whites in its councils and assemblies, this new breed of leadership was distrustful of so-called white liberals and refused to allow them to participate. Further, they cultivated the habit of prohibiting the white press from attending their meetings. Those closed meetings gradually led to the formation of black caususes within white institutions, organizations, societies, and churches.

Given our understanding of communal power and its embodiment in the black churches, it is not surprising that the black power movement was unambiguously rejected by the largest black denomination, namely, the National Baptist Convention, U.S.A., Inc., and officially ignored by all the other major black denominations. Similarly, the black churches refused to take official notice of the National Committee of Negro Churchmen (later known as the National Conference of Black Churchmen and recently renamed the National Conference of Black Christians), which attempted to provide a Christian rationale for the movement. Despite the fact that several bishops and pastors of national prominence were members of NCNC, the black churches were virtually unanimous in their suspicion of black power.

The reason for the attitude of the black denominations toward black power lies partly in the fact that the impetus for the latter came from outside the established ecclesiastical framework. Further, its language and symbols appeared to be alien to the tradition of the black churches. As a matter of fact, black power sprang from the sentiments of young black radicals in the Student Nonviolent Coordinating Committee (SNNC) who had been ardent followers of Martin Luther King, Jr., but also had been influenced considerably by various black nationalist ideologies, including that of the Nation of Islam. Any careful study of their history would reveal that the black churches have always been extremely reluctant to give official approval to any ideology or strategy that was controversial in the black community or that implicitly or explicitly attacked the black churches and their traditions.[16] Many such attacks were launched by the black power movement of the late 1960s along with the predictable responses of the black churches to them. Stereotypes and oversimplifications dominated the rhetorical outbursts of various black power leaders as they sought to criticize and chastise the traditional black leaders, who in turn were often thrown on the defensive. For a time the black community was polarized into two opposing ideological camps.

Many of the black power leaders had had limited experience with and less understanding of the black church tradition and consequently were viewed by the latter as alien forces representing dangerous understandings of power, inflammatory and abusive rhetoric, hostile dispositions, agents of potential violence, racial chauvinists, and anti-America in tastes, dress, and hairstyles. In summary, the black churches rightly perceived a movement seeking to effect a cultural revolution.

Many black religious leaders in predominantly white denominations along with others in major black denominations soon grasped the religious importance of the black power movement and attempted to express its meaning in Christian theological terms. These efforts initially culminated in a full-page statement in the *New York Times* (July 31, 1966) (see Appendix B). The statement aimed at correcting the mistaken understandings that white church leaders had of black power as a symbol of lawlessness and reverse racism. In their attempt to gain legitimation from the white churches, the drafters of the statement took great care to speak about their "beloved America" more than once. The statement constituted an argument similar to the Niebuhrian view of Christian realism in which power is understood as the capacity to get what one wants for oneself and, consequently, all should be able to exercise it lest they inherit the domination of others over themselves. Given such a reality, harmony can be attained only by a balance of powers which in history is always tenuous. Further, Niebuhr believed that power in history should be regulated by structures of justice which, in turn, should be governed by the Christian principle of love that lies beyond history. The following quotation from the statement reflected that viewpoint:

> The fundamental distortion facing us in the controversy about "black power" is rooted in a gross imbalance of power and conscience between Negroes and white Americans. It is this distortion, mainly, which is responsible for the widespread, though often inarticulate, assumption that white people are justified in getting what they want through the use of power, but that Negro Americans must, either by nature or by circumstances, make their appeal only through conscience. As a result, the power of white men and the

conscience of black men have both been corrupted. The power of white men is corrupted because it meets little meaningful resistance from Negroes to temper it and keep white men from aping God. The conscience of black men is corrupted because, having no power to implement the demands of conscience, the concern for justice is transmuted into a distorted form of love, which, in the absence of justice, becomes chaotic self-surrender. Powerlessness breeds a race of beggars. We are faced now with a situation where conscienceless power meets powerless conscience, threatening the very foundations of our nation.[17]

It is somewhat astonishing that the statement's basic argument was rooted in the black church's traditional understanding of communal power. It warned that power is not evil per se; rather, the attempt to rival God as the possessor of ultimate power is the real evil. It argued, in addition, that the problem of racism is a problem of racial inequality, and it expressed a concern for the restoration of a balance of power. This led its writers to declare, "In one sense, the concept of 'black power' reminds us of the need for and the possibility of authentic democracy in America."[18] The mutuality implicit in communal power is clearly implied by the way in which the writers related power and love. "The Negro Church was created as a result of the refusal to submit to the indignities of a false kind of 'integration' in which all power was in the hands of white people. A more equal sharing of power is precisely what is required as the precondition of authentic human interaction."[19] Further they wrote:

All people need power, whether black or white. We regard as sheer hypocrisy or as a blind and dangerous illusion the view that opposes love to power. Love should be a controlling element in power, but what love opposes is precisely the misuse and abuse of power, not power itself. So long as white churchmen continue to moralize and misinterpret Christian love, so long will justice continue to be subverted in this land.[20]

In their discussion of the relationship of power and justice the writers again seemed to envision the concept of communal power as they concluded:

We are glad that none of those civil rights leaders who have asked for "black power" have suggested that it means a new form of isola-

tionism or a foolish effort at domination. But we must be clear
about why we need be be reconciled with the white majority. . . .
   We must rather rest our concern for reconciliation on the firm
ground that we and all other Americans *are* one. Our history and
destiny are indissolubly linked. If the future is to belong to any of
us, it must be prepared for all of us whatever our racial or religious
background. For in the final analysis, we are *persons* and the power
of all groups must be wielded to make visible our common
humanity.[21]

Thus the NCNC statement on black power virtually interpreted
the concept of power in accordance with the substance of communal power. Whether or not that was totally acceptable to all the
black power advocates at the time is not so important for our purposes here. Rather, we are impressed by the fact that in their
attempt to justify black power to both the black community and
the white religious establishment, those black church leaders who
wrote the treatise called upon the resources of the black Christian
tradition to support them in their task. The outcome was an explanation of black power as communal power.

We also conclude that this outcome was no crafty form of trick-
ery. On the contrary, it represented a deep abhorrence of mere
unilateral power. As a militant agency of reform, NCNC stood in
the tradition of black Christian nationalism, à la Bishop Henry
McNeil Turner of the A.M.E. Church and Bishop Alexander
Walters of the A.M.E. Zion Church. Both these and other leaders
who concluded from time to time that blacks would never gain
equal citizenship rights in this nation continued to espouse communal power even in their call for colonization elsewhere. In short,
they were not true radicals in the sense that they advocated or participated in revolutionary attempts to grasp unilateral power
within these borders. Similarly, the black power leaders of the late
1960s and their black religious supporters were extremely militant,
but not radical. This judgment applies particularly to those who
comprised the NCNC as well as the black theology movement[22]
that it stimulated, nurtured, and promoted.

In its search for historical roots in the black American experience, the black power movement could find very little that stood
in radical isolation from the values of the black Christian tradi-

tion. In fact, its search for historical roots was tantamount to a declaration that it was not a revolutionary movement, its rhetoric notwithstanding. Its informal adoption of the NAACP's anthem (traditionally called the "Negro's National Anthem") reinforced this viewpoint, since the anthem's religious and political grounding is unmistakably in the black Christian tradition, including the ambiguity that attends the term "native land"—clearly enabling either an American or an African patriotism which thereby reconciles both the right and left wings of the black community.

> God of our weary years, God of our silent tears,
> God who has brought us thus far on the way.
> God who has by Thy might led us into the light,
> Keep us forever in the path, we pray.
> Lest our feet stray from the places, our God, where we
>   met Thee,
> Lest our hearts, drunk with the wine of the world, we
>   forget Thee;
> Shadowed beneath Thy hand, May we forever stand,
> True to our God, True to our native land.

Black power's persistent attempts to develop a sense of continuity with African cultural traditions were destined to become an experience in racial romanticism, since those efforts were rooted in little knowledge and less experience of Africa. Nevertheless, the event of the black power movement produced some lasting effects that have been and continue to be enormously important because they have been correctives to the weaknesses intrinsic in communal power. Some of these effects are: (1) the term "black" has become universally accepted by black Americans as their preferred name for the race, and such former terms as "Negro" and "colored" have been retired to the dustbins of history; (2) a new sense of pride in black identity, African heritage, and Afro-American history; (3) a significant psychological and cultural decrease in the race's sense of inferiority; (4) an increased capacity for the pursuit of racial self-interest; (5) a growing appreciation of racial, ethnic, and cultural pluralism as harmonious with a racially integrated society.

The impact of black power has contributed significantly to the race's self-understanding of communal power by enabling the race to see the dangers implicit in any tendency to disregard the needs and the capacities of the self in its efforts to effect community. Similarly, the efforts of black religionists to interpret black power as harmonious with communal power served to check and balance its tendency to destroy community in its pursuit of unilateral power. In short, each is a corrective on the other. Apart from unilateral power, communal power tends toward self-impoverishment, and without communal power unilateral power tends toward the destruction of the other. Both tendencies destroy the possibility for community.

In the present day, blacks in general and the black churches in particular have become less reluctant to pursue their own racial self-interest. Clearly, they have a long history of such pursuits. The only difference is that they now display less anxiety concerning them. That is to say, they are less preoccupied with whether or not certain kinds of advocacy will make them appear racist. This may in part be attributed to a wider acceptance of ethnic group pluralism in present-day America than was formerly the case. Certainly the effect of the black power movement has had no small amount of influence on this current state of affairs.

NOTES

1. George A. Singleton, *The Romance of African Methodism* (New York: Exposition Press, 1952), 177.

2. See Carter G. Woodson, *The History of the Negro Church*, 3rd ed. (Washington, D.C.: Associated Publishers, 1972), 35ff.

3. E. Franklin Frazier, *The Negro Church in America* (New York: Schocken Books, 1964), 16.

4. Albert J. Raboteau, *Slave Religion: The "Invisible Institution" in the Antebellum South* (New York: Oxford University Press, 1980), 219.

5. Benjamin E. Mays and Joseph W. Nicholson, *The Negro's Church* (New York: Institute of Social and Religious Research, 1933), 278ff.

6. We contend that the black independent churches have contributed indirectly to the capacity of those blacks in predominantly white denominations to sustain their association therein, an association which in part is enabled by the microcosmic experience of independence they experience in predominantly black congregations within those denominations.

7. Whenever blacks are asked what they want they usually respond in

such a way as to reveal that they desire whatever whites have by way of rights, demands, opportunities, status, acceptance, and the like. Whenever the black churches advocate racial equality they express the deepest longings of the race. Further, whenever any persons or groups in the white community become spokespersons for racial equality, they inevitably gain the respect of blacks. And that respect is never misplaced, since whites advocate racial equality so seldom; and since the implications of doing so are so serious, blacks have rarely experienced the betrayal of such persons.

8. Martin E. Marty, "Religious Power in America: A Contemporary Map," in *Criterion* 21, no. 1 (Winter 1982), 30–31.

9. In the latter half of the twentieth century the race problem in America has assumed a more unified national form than in previous generations. Formerly, the forces of racial justice were able to capitalize on antiregional sentiments in the formation of their alliances, especially since the form of racism they were combating (namely Jim Crowism) was largely southern in its most blatant expressions. Since that is no longer the case, it remains for the future to determine whether or not the problem will be more difficult to correct.

10. For this insight as well as significant parts of this chapter, I am indebted to Prof. Bernard Loomer and, in particular, to his essay "Two Kinds of Power" (see the D. R. Sharpe Lectureship on Social Ethics: The Inauguration and First Lecture, in *Criterion* 15, no. 1 (Winter 1976), 12–29.

11. William J. Walls, *The African Methodist Episcopal Zion Church: Reality of the Black Church* (Charlotte, N.C.: A.M.E. Zion Church Publishing House, 1974), 533.

12. The African Orthodox Church of the Marcus Garvey movement and the Church of the Black Madonna begun by Albert Cleage are two such examples.

13. C. Eric Lincoln, *The Black Church Since Frazier* (New York: Schocken Books, 1974).

14. Gayraud S. Wilmore, *Black Religion and Black Radicalism* (New York: Doubleday & Co., 1972) chap. 8.

15. Ibid., 263, 264–65.

16. At the turn of the century it was the Women's Auxiliary of the National Baptist Convention that took the initiative to invite Booker T. Washington and W. E. B. DuBois to their convention. They did so because they felt that the leaders of the convention feared too greatly the consequences of extending invitations to such controversial figures.

17. "Black Power: A Statement by the National Committee of Negro Churchmen, July 31, 1966," in Nathan Wright, Jr., *Black Power and Urban Unrest* (New York: Hawthorn Books, 1967), 187. It should not be surprising that the argument of this statement should be Niebuhrian in style, since the latter has dominated the social thinking of the mainline

white American churches for over three decades and many of the black leaders who signed the statement had been influenced by that style both in their theological education as well as the white ecclesiastical contexts in which they were carrying out their respective ministries.

18. Ibid., 189.

19. Ibid., 188–89.

20. Ibid., 190.

21. Ibid., 191–92.

22. The response of the black churches to the black theology movement, of which James H. Cone was the chief systematician and progenitor, has been similar in all respects to their response to black power and the NCNC. As they had rejected Marcus Garvey's African Orthodox Church because of the place of prominence it gave to race consciousness and its propositions that God is black, (and, accordingly, its demands that the churches be purged of pictures of white Madonnas and the baby Jesus), so also they rejected black theology. Further, the black churches could never condone the tendency of the black power movement to set forth violence as a veiled threat, a practice that black theology justified under the principle of self-defense.

Conclusion

We began this study with an analysis of the circumstances that led to the emergence of the black church independence movement — a socioreligious event that began to assume institutional expression in the late eighteenth century. Our inquiry has shown that the major objective of that movement was the institutionalization of the Christian faith in a nonracist form. We conclude that that goal alone has constituted the final aim and purpose of the black churches. Although it was variously expressed in both religious symbols and political concepts, we have shown that their nonracist appropriation of the Christian faith was grounded in a biblical anthropology derivative from the principle of the parenthood of God and the kinship of all peoples. In brief, the life and the mission of the black churches have been integrally related to that principle apart from which there would have been no need for their separate existence then or now and under which everything else in the churches has been rendered subordinate, including all questions of doctrine, polity, and liturgy. Hence we conclude that since the Christian faith has been viewed by blacks as nonracist, and since they have sought to institutionalize that view in their churches, and since that effort has constituted their distinctive and unique contribution to the Christian faith, there is therefore no distinction between black Methodists and black Baptists that equals or supersedes that principle. Rather, that which makes the churches either Methodist or Baptist is subordinate to their commitment to the parenthood of God and the kinship of all people, which alone constitutes the essence of the black Christian tradition.

The commitment of the black churches to their peculiar tradition, however, has not lessened their commitment to the basic principles of their nation. During much of their history they have assumed that the nation's racism was changeable, and that fact has shaped their disposition as well as their methods for effecting the desired social changes. Accordingly, much of this study has sought to describe the nature of the moral conflicts that have permeated the life of the black churches in their efforts to reform the larger society as patriotic moral agents desirous of full participation in the public life of the nation. Further, we have argued that the black churches have never equated the nation with evil itself and hence have never understood their struggle for racial justice as a "holy war" in spite of their certainty concerning the rightness of their cause. For reasons that must be left to another kind of inquiry, blacks have always had a high level of commitment to the fundamental principles underlying the American republic. Although they have always been aware of the ubiquity of racism that permeates all dimensions of the nation's life, they have refrained from making radical moral judgments about the nation's ideals (that is, the constitution) and its practices. Rather, the understandings and actions of the black churches have assumed that a dilemma exists between the nation's ideals and practices, and that stance has enabled them to believe in the changeability of those practices by moral suasion, legislation, and enforcement. Because of their primacy in the black community, the churches have had immense influence in shaping the basic values of the black community in accordance with their own understandings. Hence we assume a direct correlation between the political posture of the black churches and the lack of political radicalism in the black community. Nevertheless, in the light of the prevailing American ethos governing race relations, we contend that the principle that the black churches have sought to institutionalize has always implied radically different social and political arrangements. In other words, their aim of transforming a racist society into a nonracist society implied a radical cultural transformation.

But the churches chose to employ lawful and moderate strategies for the achievement of these radical ends, and that has constituted a predominant dilemma in their thought and action.

This study demonstrates the many and varied moral and political conflicts that have attended the history of the black churches — conflicts emergent from the peculiar relationship the black churches have had both to the nation and to the race. These conflicts have been rooted in the heart of the black churches — their commitment to the nation, on the one hand, and their loyalty to the race, on the other; the limiting impact of their societal vision on racial development by subordinating the latter as a means to an end rather than an end consistent with that vision; the concomitant impact of that vision on the political life of the black churches and their failure to discern a positive relationship between political realism and political idealism as well as their interest in exploring the relationship of socioreligious thought and sociological location and the ways in which both are instrumental in shaping institutions and their activities. Finally, the various ambiguities implicit in their autonomy, moral agency, and political wisdom have led to an understanding of power that has distinguished the churches from the rest of American life in general. Hence it was not surprising to see the uneasiness the black churches felt with the idea of black power and its implications for theology, ethics, and politics.

At each point this inquiry has sought to maintain a close relationship to the representative thought and activity of the black denominations. Clarification of actual conflicts in thought and practice has been our aim. Our generalizations pertain to the denominations under study and only hypothetically to other black churches. Thus we have refrained as much as possible from dealing with abstract ideas, principles, and concepts. Rather, we have tried to concentrate our focus on the actual thought of the denominations and their leaders. Accordingly, our method has compelled us to reflect on the actual desires and intentions of real associations possessing varying capacities for deliberating and choosing among alternative possibilities. Further, we have discerned in the literature of the churches a very low level of institutional self-criticism

132 Conclusion

about either their purpose or the nature of their activities aimed at social reform. Like all institutions, the black churches have become firmly routinized in their traditions and consequently strongly resistant to internal change. A high level of devotion to their traditions and the preservation of these traditions characterizes much of the life of the churches at the denominational levels. Their capacity to encourage and to receive rigorous self-criticism in the light of their real desires remains unclear.

In our day various activities in the black community at large (and especially in those interracial associations and institutions including black churches in predominantly white denominations) are motivated by racial self-interest in a new way. That is to say, blacks generally no longer feel that they are betraying their ideal societal vision by working vigorously for such racial goals as political determination, economic development, preservation of predominantly black schools (private and public), construction of senior citizens homes in the black community. While all blacks would oppose racial proscription in any form, in these post–Jim Crow days growing numbers of blacks see no inherent moral problem with the pursuit of race interests. Clearly this represents a change in the times. In a former day such pursuit could easily have implied some form of accommodationism to the prevailing ethos of racial discrimination and segregation. But in our day the law is clearly opposed to these practices, and consequently, like many immigrant groups that have maintained a high level of group consciousness in their pursuit of cultural, political, economic and social value, many blacks now feel free to do likewise. This tendency was evidenced in the successful bid of the Honorable Walter Fauntroy, a black Baptist clergyman in Washington, D.C., when, in 1972, he became the first nonvoting congressional delegate representing the District of Columbia. Similarly, the Reverend Jesse Jackson appeals to the same values in his race to become the Democratic Party's candidate for president of the United States. Nevertheless, in the main the denominations have been reluctant in either thought or action to express their views on the phenomenon of cultural pluralism and its implications for the religion, morality, and politics of blacks in general and themselves in particular.

The significance of this study for religious social ethics is multi-faceted. First, it has been an inquiry into the way in which black religious institutions have sought to relate themselves to the larger white society. This investigation has laid the basis for comparative analyses with other racial minorities in similar circumstances — for example, native-born black Canadians; West Indians in Canada, England, and France; citizens of African descent in Brazil and elsewhere in South America; and Native Americans and Hispanics in the United States. Such comparative analyses would determine the extent to which we can generalize about the religious and moral experience of racially oppressed minorities.

Second, our inquiry has comprised a study of the internal relationship of church and society in the black community and the way in which each has been a necessary condition of the other. In doing so, we have shown that the social teaching of the black churches not only expresses the sociological and political dimensions of the black churches but also has shaped both their internal life and external mission. Since the black churches have comprised the institutional center of the black community, we conclude that their predominant responses to the nation's racism reveals paradigms of thought and action that have become normative for the black community at large.

Third, we have shown that the black churches and the white churches differ from each other in their respective purposes despite their many similarities in doctrine and polity. Hence that which separates the black churches from the white churches, namely, black opposition to the racism of the other, is also the principle of unity among black churches and throughout the black community.

At one time black churches were viewed (especially by whites) as otherworldly and escapist institutions reflecting the despair of the black community and/or manifesting themselves as poor replicas of white churches. The revisionist black scholarship of the past two decades has helped change that misconception. As a result, the black churches are no longer viewed primarily as defective institutions merely because they differ from white churches. Also, increasingly, they are no longer being understood merely as social institutions with political and psychological import, but as religious institutions. Implicit in this viewpoint is the understanding that the religious content of the black churches (as well as that of all churches) must be grasped and developed within a historical context, because even that which transcends history is dependent upon history for its transmission. In other words, there can be no sharp cleavage between the substance of religion and that of historical experience. Further, we conclude that black perceptions about the relevance and immediacy of Christianity to their social condition need not imply any threat to its universality. In fact, the principle idea the black churches sought to institutionalize—the parenthood of God and the kinship of all peoples—was not the creation of the black churches themselves. They merely sought the means of embodying it in their practice and as a moral claim on white churches to affirm in thought and practice the "kinship of all peoples" as the practical inference of the "parenthood of God." Their faithfulness to what we have called "the black Christian tradition" has enabled the black churches to stand as manifestations of the universal truth that Christianity purportedly has sought to reveal. Hence to call them race institutions is only a half-truth. In fact, it may imply a dangerous misconception of their nature. More accurately, the black churches represent in their thought and disposition the universality of Christianity manifested in the midst of racial particularity. Their primary mission has always been that of calling the nation to effect racial equality and justice (that is, the kinship of all peoples) within its borders. As we have said previously, the formation of separate black churches has never been viewed as fully satisfying by blacks because of their great difficulty in relating it positively to their ideal societal vision. Nevertheless, as lure and judge, that vision has inspired their love of racial unity and enabled them to cultivate moral support for social transformation as a condition for interracial unity. But devotion to that vision has restrained their efforts toward racial self-development.

The African Methodist Social Creed

1. We believe that the universal laws of God supercedes all human devices for peaceful relations among men and nations, and that man's first loyalty is to God and his conscience.
2. We believe in the dignity of man and in the sacredness of human personality and we regard as the most enlightened steps in social progress those political teachings which recognize these basic concepts.
3. We believe in the oneness of the human race.
4. We believe that marriage is more than a social contract, and that it was ordained by God, and, therefore, is sacred and honorable.
5. We believe that only adultery on the part of either husband or wife is ground for divorce.
6. We believe racial prejudices and discrimination in all forms to be injurious to the unity of mankind.
7. We believe that all members of the human family should be accorded equal opportunities for educational, social, and cultural development in accordance with their capacities and inclinations.
8. We believe that men under all forms of government should be given the right of freedom of speech and of worship, and these rights ought never be denied or abridged by any state or nation.
9. We believe that no man should be denied his right to earn a living because of race, creed, or color.

10. We believe the individual ownership of property is in accord with Christian principles and should be encouraged and used in the light of Christian Stewardship. We believe in collective bargaining and social action on the part of employer and employee alike.

11. We believe in the New Testament principle of Temperance, and, therefore, regard the use of alcohol as a beverage and dope as moral and social evils.

12. We believe that through faith in the Lord Jesus Christ, the minds and spirits of men may be transformed by the bestowal of the Holy Spirit, and the grace to return good for evil and patience to employ non-violent methods to obtain just and lasting peace.

13. We reaffirm our belief in the Protestant principle of the separation of church and state.

14. We believe in the unity of all Christian believers, particularly those of African descent who are members of Methodist bodies, and prayerfully look forward to the day when all will be one.

15. We believe in the redeemability of sinful humanity through belief in the teachings of Jesus Christ concerning the universality of the Fatherhood of God, and the brotherhood of man.

16. Upon the adoption of this Creed by the General Conference, the Bishops' Council recommends that an annual reading of this Social Creed in all our churches and Sunday Schools be made by the pastor, or someone selected by him.

APPENDIX **B**

"Black Power"

A STATEMENT BY THE NATIONAL
COMMITTEE OF NEGRO CHURCHMEN
July 31, 1966

We, an informal group of Negro churchmen in America, are deeply disturbed about the crisis brought upon our country by historic distortions of important human realities in the controversy about "black power." What we see shining through the variety of rhetoric is not anything new but the same old problem of power and race which has faced our beloved country since 1619.

We realize that neither the term "power" nor the term "Christian Conscience" is an easy matter to talk about, especially in the context of race relations in America. The fundamental distortion facing us in the controversy about "black power" is rooted in a gross imbalance of power and conscience between Negroes and white Americans. It is this distortion, mainly, which is responsible for the widespread, though often inarticulate, assumption that white people are justified in getting what they want through the use of power, but that Negro Americans must, either by nature or by circumstances, make their appeal only through conscience. As a result, the power of white men and the conscience of black men have both been corrupted. The power of white men is corrupted because it meets little meaningful resistance from Negroes to temper it and keep white men from aping God. The conscience of black men is corrupted because, having no power to implement the demands of conscience, the concern for justice is transmuted into a distorted form of love, which, in the absence of justice,

137

becomes chaotic self-surrender. Powerlessness breeds a race of beggars. We are faced now with a situation where conscienceless power meets powerless conscience, threatening the very foundations of our nation.

Therefore, we are impelled by conscience to address at least four groups of people in areas where clarification of the controversy is of the most urgent necessity. We do not claim to present the final word. It is our hope, however, to communicate meanings from our experience regarding power and certain elements of conscience to help interpret more adequately the dilemma in which we are all involved.

I. To the Leaders of America: Power and Freedom

It is of critical importance that the leaders of this nation listen also to a voice which says that the principal source of the threat to our nation comes neither from the riots erupting in our big cities, nor from the disagreements among the leaders of the civil rights movement, nor even from mere raising of the cry of "black power." These events, we believe, are but the expression of the judgment of God upon our nation for its failure to use its abundant resources to serve the real well-being of people, at home and abroad.

We give our full support to all civil rights leaders as they seek for basically American goals, for we are not convinced that their mutual reinforcement of one another in the past is bound to end in the future. We would hope that the public power of our nation will be used to strengthen the civil rights movement and not to manipulate or further fracture it.

We deplore the overt violence of riots, but we believe it is more important to focus on the real sources of these eruptions. These sources may be abetted inside the ghetto, but their basic causes lie in the silent and covert violence which white middle-class America inflicts upon the victims of the inner city. The hidden, smooth and often smiling decisions of American leaders which tie a white noose of suburbia around the necks, and which pin the backs of the masses of Negroes against the steaming ghetto walls—without jobs in a booming economy; with dilapidated and segregated educational systems in the full view of unenforced laws against it; in short: the failure of American leaders to use American power to create equal opportunity *in life* as well as *in law* — this is the real problem and not the anguished cry for "black power."

From the point of view of the Christian faith, there is nothing necessarily wrong with concern for power. At the heart of the Protestant reformation is the belief that ultimate power belongs to God alone and that men become most inhuman when concentrations of power lead to the conviction — overt or covert — that any nation, race or organization can rival God in this regard. At issue in the relations between whites and Negroes in America is the problem of inequality of power. Out of this imbalance grows the disrespect of white men for the Negro personality and community, and the disrespect of Negroes for themselves. This is a fundamental root of human injustice in America. In one sense, the concept of "black power" reminds us of the need for and the possibility of authentic democracy in America.

We do *not* agree with those who say that we must cease expressing concern for the acquisition of power lest we endanger the "gains" already made by the civil rights movement. The fact of the matter is, there have been few substantive gains since about 1950 in this area. The gap has constantly widened between the incomes of non-whites relative to the whites. Since the Supreme Court decision of 1954, de facto segregation in every major city in our land has increased rather than decreased. Since the middle of the 1950s unemployment among Negroes has gone up rather than down while unemployment has decreased in the white community.

While there has been some progress in some areas for equality for Negroes, this progress has been limited mainly to middle-class Negroes who represent only a small minority of the larger Negro community.

These are the hard facts that we must all face together. Therefore, we must not take the position that we can continue in the same old paths.

When American leaders decide to serve the real welfare of people instead of war and destruction; when American leaders are forced to make the rebuilding of our cities first priority on the nation's agenda; when American leaders are forced by the American people to quit misusing and abusing American power; then will the cry for "black power" become inaudible, for the framework in which all power in America operates would include the power and experience of black men as well as those of white men. In that way, the fear of the power of each group would be removed. America is our beloved homeland. But, America is not God. Only God can do everything. America and the other nations of the world must decide which among a number of alternatives they will choose.

II. To White Churchmen: Power and Love

As black men who were long ago forced out of the white church to create and to wield "black power," we fail to understand the emotional quality of the outcry of some clergy against the use of the term today. It is not enough to answer that "integration" is the solution. For it is precisely the nature of the operation of power under some forms of integration which is being challenged. The Negro Church was created as a result of the refusal to submit to the indignities of a false kind of "integration" in which all power was in the hands of white people. A more equal sharing of power is precisely what is required as the precondition of authentic human interaction. We understand the growing demand of Negro and white youth for a more honest kind of integration; one which increases rather than decreases the capacity of the disinherited to participate with power in all of the structures of our common life. Without this capacity to *participate with power*—i.e., to have some organized political and economic strength to really influence people with whom one interacts—integration is not meaningful. For the issue is not one of racial balance but of honest interracial interaction.

For this kind of interaction to take place, all people need power, whether black or white. We regard as sheer hypocrisy or as a blind and dangerous illusion the view that opposes love to power. Love should be a controlling element in power, but what love opposes is precisely the misuse and abuse of power, not power itself. So long as white churchmen continue to moralize and misinterpret Christian love, so long will justice continue to be subverted in this land.

III. To Negro Citizens: Power and Justice

Both the anguished cry for "black power" and the confused emotional response to it can be understood if the whole controversy is put in the context of American history. Especially must we understand the irony involved in the pride of Americans regarding their ability to act as individuals on the one hand, and their tendency to act as members of ethnic groups on the other hand. In the tensions of this part of our history is revealed both the tragedy and the hope of human redemption in America.

America has asked its Negro citizens to fight for opportunity *as individuals* whereas at certain points in our history what we have needed most has been opportunity for the whole group, not just for selected and approved Negroes. Thus in 1863, the slaves were made legally free, as individuals, but the real question regarding personal and group power to maintain that freedom was pushed aside. Power at that time for a mainly rural people meant land and tools to work the land. In the words of Thaddeus Stevens, power meant "40 acres and a mule." But this power was not made available to the slaves and we see the results today in the pushing of a landless peasantry off the farms into big cities where they come in search mainly of the power to be free. What they find are only the formalities of unenforced legal freedom. So we must ask, "what is the nature of the power which we seek and need today?" Power today is essentially organizational power. It is not a thing lying about in the streets to be fought over. It is a thing which, in some measure, already belongs to Negroes and which must be developed by Negroes in relationship with the great resources of this nation.

Getting power necessarily involves reconciliation. We must first be reconciled to ourselves lest we fail to recognize the resources we already have and upon which we can build. We must be reconciled to ourselves as persons and to ourselves as an historical group. This means we must find our way to a new self-image in which we can feel a normal sense of pride in self, including our variety of skin color and the manifold textures of our hair. As long as we are filled with hatred for ourselves we will be unable to respect others.

At the same time, if we are seriously concerned about power then we must build upon that which we already have. "Black power" is already present to some extent in the Negro church, in Negro fraternities and sororities, in our professional associations, and in the opportunities afforded to Negroes who make decisions in some of the integrated organizations of our society.

We understand the reasons by which these limited forms of "black power" have been rejected by some of our people. Too often the Negro church has stirred its members away from the reign of God in *this world* to a distorted and complacent view of *an other-worldly* conception of God's power. We commit ourselves as churchmen to make more meaningful in the life of our institution our conviction that Jesus Christ reigns in the "here" and "now" as well as in the future he brings in upon us. We shall, therefore, use more of the resources of our churches in working for human justice in the places of social change and upheaval where our Master is already at work.

At the same time, we would urge that Negro social and professional organizations develop new roles for engaging the problem of equal opportunity and put less time into the frivolity of idle chatter and social waste.

We must not apologize for the existence of this form of group power, for we have been oppressed as a group, not as individuals. We will not find our way out of that oppression until both we and America accept the need for Negro Americans as well as for Jews, Italians, Poles and White Anglo-Saxon Protestants, among others, to have and to wield group power.

However, if power is sought merely as an end in itself, it tends to turn upon those who seek it. Negroes need power in order to participate more effectively at all levels of the life of our nation. We are glad that none of those civil rights leaders who have asked for "black power" have suggested that it means a new form of isolationism or a foolish effort at domination. But we must be clear about why we need to be reconciled with the white majority. It is *not* because we are only one-tenth of the population in

America; for we do not need to be reminded of the awesome power wielded by the 90% majority. We see and feel that power every day in the destruction heaped upon our families and upon the nation's cities. We do not need to be threatened by such cold and heartless statements. For we are men, not children, and we are growing out of our fear of that power, which can hardly hurt us any more in the future than it does in the present or has in the past. Moreover, those bare figures conceal the potential political strength which is ours if we organize properly in the big cities and establish effective alliances.

Neither must we rest our concern for reconciliation with our white brothers on the fear that failure to do so would damage gains already made by the civil rights movement. If those gains are in fact real, they will withstand the claims of our people for power and justice, not just for a few select Negroes here and there, but for the masses of our citizens. We must rather rest our concern for reconciliation on the firm ground that we and all other Americans *are* one. Our history and destiny are indissolubly linked. If the future is to belong to any of us, it must be prepared for all of us whatever our racial or religious background. For in the final analysis, we are *persons* and the power of all groups must be wielded to make visible our common humanity.

The future of America will belong to neither white nor black unless all Americans work together at the task of rebuilding our cities. We must organize not only among ourselves but with other groups in order that we can, together, gain power sufficient to change this nation's sense of what is *now* important and what must be done *now*. We must work with the remainder of the nation to organize whole cities for the task of making the rebuilding of our cities first priority in the use of our resources. This is more important than who gets to the moon first or the war in Vietnam.

To accomplish this task we cannot expend our energies in spastic or ill-tempered explosions without meaningful goals. We must move from the politics of philanthropy to the politics of metropolitan development for equal opportunity. We must relate all groups of the city together in new ways in order that the truth of our cities might be laid bare and in order that, together, we can lay claim to the great resources of our nation to make truth more human.

IV. To the Mass Media: Power and Truth

The ability of all people in America to understand the upheavals of our day depends greatly on the way power and truth operate in the mass media. During the Southern demonstrations for civil rights, you men of the communications industry performed an invaluable service for the entire country by revealing plainly to our ears and eyes, the ugly truth of a brutalizing system of overt discrimination and segregation. Many of you were mauled and injured, and it took courage for you to stick with the task. You were instruments of change and not merely purveyors of unrelated facts. You were able to do this by dint of personal courage and by reason of the power of national news agencies which supported you.

Today, however, your task and ours is more difficult. The truth that needs revealing today is not so clear-cut in its outlines, nor is there a national consenus to help you form relevant points of view. Therefore, nothing is now more important than that you look for a variety of sources of truth in order that the limited perspectives of all of us might be corrected. Just as you related to a broad spectrum of people in Mississippi instead of relying only on police records and establishment figures, so must you operate in New York City, Chicago, and Cleveland.

The power to support you in this endeavor *is present* in our country. It must be searched out. We desire to use our limited influence to help relate you to the variety of experience in the Negro community so that limited controversies are not blown up into the final truth about us. The fate of this country is, to no small extent, dependent upon how you interpret the crises upon us, so that human truth is disclosed and human needs are met.

SIGNATORIES

Bishop John D. Bright, Sr., AME Church, First Episcopal District, Philadelphia, Pennsylvania

The Rev. John Bryan, Connecticut Council of Churches, Hartford, Connecticut

Suffragan Bishop John M. Burgess, The Episcopal Church, Boston, Massachusetts

The Rev. W. Sterling Cary, Grace Congregational Church, New York, New York

The Rev. Charles E. Cobb, St. John Church (UCC), Springfield, Massachusetts

The Rev. Caesar D. Coleman, Christian Methodist Episcopal Church, Memphis, Tennessee

The Rev. Joseph C. Coles, Williams Institutional C.M.E. Church, New York, New York

The Rev. George A. Crawley, Jr., St. Paul Baptist Church, Baltimore, Maryland

The Rev. O. Herbert Edwards, Trinity Baptist Church, Baltimore, Maryland

The Rev. Bryant George, United Presbyterian Church in the U.S.A., New York, New York

Bishop Charles F. Golden, The Methodist Church, Nashville, Tennessee

The Rev. Quinland R. Gordon, The Episcopal Church, New York, New York

The Rev. James Hargett, Church of Christian Fellowship, U.C.C., Los Angeles, California

The Rev. Edler Hawkins, St. Augustine Presbyterian Church, New York, New York

The Rev. Reginald Hawkins, United Presbyterian Church, Charlotte, North Carolina

Dr. Anna Arnold Hedgeman, Commission on Religion and Race, National Council of Churches, New York, New York

The Rev. R. E. Hood, Gary, Indiana

The Rev. H. R. Hughes, Bethel A.M.E. Church, New York, New York

The Rev. Kenneth Hughes, St. Bartholomew's Episcopal Church, Cambridge, Massachusetts

The Rev. Donald G. Jacobs, St. James A.M.E. Church, Cleveland, Ohio

The Rev. J. L. Joiner, Emanuel A.M.E. Church, New York, New York

The Rev. Arthur A. Jones, Metropolitan A.M.E. Church, Philadelphia, Pennsylvania

The Rev. Stanley King, Sabathini Baptist Church, Minneapolis, Minnesota

The Rev. Earl Wesley Lawson, Emanuel Baptist Church, Malden, Massachusetts

The Rev. David Licorish, Abyssinian Baptist Church, New York, New York

The Rev. Arthur B. Mack, St. Thomas A.M.E.Z. Church, Haverstraw, New York

The Rev. James W. Mack, South United Church of Christ, Chicago, Illinois

The Rev. O. Clay Maxwell, Jr., Baptist Ministers Conference of New York City and Vicinity, New York, New York

The Rev. Leon Modeste, the Episcopal Church, New York, New York

Bishop Noah W. Moore, Jr., The Methodist Church, Southwestern Area, Houston, Texas

The Rev. David Nickerson, Episcopal Society for Cultural and

Racial Unity, Atlanta, Georgia

The Rev. LeRoy Patrick, Bethesda United Presbyterian Church, Pittsburgh, Pennsylvania

The Rev. Benjamin F. Payton, Commission on Religion and Race, National Council of Churches, New York, New York

The Rev. Isaiah P. Pogue, St. Mark's Presbyterian Church, Cleveland, Ohio

The Rev. Sandy F. Ray, Empire Baptist State Convention, Brooklyn, New York

Bishop Herbert B. Shaw, Presiding Bishop, Third Episcopal District, A.M.E.Z. Church, Wilmington, North Carolina

The Rev. Stephen P. Spottswood, Commission on Race and Cultural Relations, Detroit Council of Churches, Detroit, Michigan

The Rev. Henri A. Stines, Church of the Atonement, Washington, D.C.

Bishop James S. Thomas, Resident Bishop, Iowa Area, The Methodist Church, Des Moines, Iowa

The Rev. V. Simpson Turner, Mt. Carmel Baptist Church, Brooklyn, New York

The Rev. Edgar Ward, Grace Presbyterian Church, Chicago, Illinois

The Rev. Paul M. Washington, Church of the Advocate, Philadelphia, Pennsylvania

The Rev. Frank L. Williams, Methodist Church, Baltimore, Maryland

The Rev. John W. Williams, St. Stephen's Baptist Church, Kansas City, Missouri

The Rev. Gayraud Wilmore, United Presbyterian Church U.S.A., New York, New York

The Rev. M. L. Wilson, Covenant Baptist Church, New York, New York

The Rev. Robert H. Wilson, Corresponding Secretary, National Baptist Convention of America, Dallas, Texas

The Rev. Nathan Wright, Episcopal Diocese of Newark, Newark, New Jersey

(Organizational affiliation given for identification purposes only.)

Bibliography

This bibliography lists only works directly referred to or quoted from in the text.

Aptheker, Herbert, ed. *A Documentary History of the Negro People in the United States.* Vol. 2. New York: Citadel Press, 1964.

Bradley, David Henry, Jr., *A History of the A.M.E. Zion Church. Vol. 2, 1872–1968.* Nashville: Parthenon Press, 1970.

Carroll, H. K.; Harrison, W. P.; Bayliss, J. H., eds. *Proceedings, Sermons, Essays and Addresses of the Centennial Methodist Conference held in the Mount Vernon Place Methodist Episcopal Church, Baltimore, Md., December 9–17, 1884.* New York: Phillips and Hunt, 1885.

Cone, James H. *Black Theology and Black Power.* New York: Seabury Press, 1969.

————. *God of the Oppressed.* New York: Seabury Press, 1975.

————. *The Spirituals and the Blues.* New York: Seabury Press, 1972.

Drake, St. Clair, and Clayton, Horace R. *Black Metropolis: A Study of Negro Life in a Northern City.* Vol. 2. New York: Harper & Row, 1962.

DuBois, W. E. B. *The Souls of Black Folk.* In *Three Negro Classics.* New York: Avon Books, 1965.

Essien-Udom, E. U. *Black Nationalism: A Search for an Identity in America.* New York: Dell Publishing Co., 1965.

Fisher, Miles Mark. *Negro Slave Songs in the United States.* New York: Citadel Press, 1969.

Fordham, Monroe. *Major Themes in Northern Black Religious Thought, 1800–1860.* New York: Exposition Press, 1975.

Franklin, John Hope. *From Slavery to Freedom.* New York: Alfred A. Knopf, 1947.

Frazier, E. Franklin. *Black Bourgeoisie.* New York: Free Press, 1957.

———. *The Negro Church in America*. New York: Schocken Books, 1964.

Gaines, Wesley J. *African Methodism in the South; or, Twenty-five Years of Freedom*. Chicago: Afro-Am Press, 1969.

Genovese, Eugene D. *Roll, Jordan, Roll: The World the Slaves Made*. New York: Pantheon Books, 1974.

George, Carol V. R. *Segregated Sabbaths: Richard Allen and the Emergence of Independent Black Churches, 1760–1840*. New York: Oxford University Press, 1973.

Glazer, Nathan. "Politics of a Multiethnic Society." In *Ethnic Relations in America*, edited by Lance Liebman. New York: Prentice-Hall, 1982.

Haley, James T. *Afro-American Encyclopaedia; or, The Thoughts, Doings and Sayings of the Race*. Nashville: Haley and Florida, 1896.

Harding, Vincent. "Religion and Resistance Among Antebellum Negroes." In *The Making of Black America: Essays in Negro Life and History*, edited by August Meier and Elliott Rudwick, vol. 1. New York: Atheneum Publishers, 1969.

Jenifer, John Thomas. *Centennial Retrospect: History of the A.M.E. Church*. Nashville: Sunday School Union Print, 1915.

Jones Lawrence. "Black Churches in Historical Perspective." In *Christianity and Crisis*, 30, no. 18 (November 12 and 16, 1970).

Jordan, L. G. *Negro Baptist History U.S.A., 1750–1930*. Nashville: Sunday School Publishing Board, 1930.

Lanternari, Vittorio. *The Religions of the Oppressed: A Study of Modern Messianic Cults*. New York: Alfred A. Knopf, 1963.

Lincoln, C. Eric. *The Black Church Since Frazier*. New York: Schocken Books, 1974.

Long, Charles H. "Assessment and New Departures for a Study of Black Religion in the United States of America." In *Black Religious Scholarship: Reflection and Promise*. Addresses delivered at the 10th Annual Meeting of the Society for the Study of Black Religion, New York City, October 22–24, 1981.

Loomer, Bernard. "Two Kinds of Power." In *Criterion*, 15, no. 1 (Winter 1976).

Marty, Martin E. "Religious Power in America: A Contemporary Map." In *Criterion*, 21, no. 1 (Winter 1982).

Mays, Benjamin E. *The Negro's God as Reflected in His Literature*. New York: Atheneum Publishers, 1968.

Mays, Benjamin E., and Nicholson, Joseph W. *The Negro's Church*. New York: Institute of Social and Religious Research, 1933.

Morris, E. C. *Sermons, Addresses and Reminiscences and Important Correspondence with a Picture Gallery of Eminent Ministers and Scholars*. Nashville: National Baptist Publishing Board, 1901.

Myrdal, Gunnar. *An American Dilemma.* Vol. 2. New York: Harper & Brothers, 1944.

Niebuhr, H. Richard. *Social Sources of Denominationalism.* New York: World Publishing Co., 1972.

Paris, Peter J. *Black Leaders in Conflict.* New York: Pilgrim Press, 1978.

Parsons, Talcott. "Full Citizenship for the Negro American?" In *The Negro American,* edited by Talcott Parsons and Kenneth B. Clark. Cambridge, Mass.: Houghton Mifflin Co., 1966.

Payne, Daniel Alexander. *Recollections of Seventy Years.* New York: Arno Press and the New York Times Co., 1968.

———. *Sermons and Addresses 1853–1891.* New York: Arno Press, 1972.

Raboteau, Albert J. *Slave Religion: The "Invisible Institution" in the Antebellum South.* New York: Oxford University Press, 1978.

Ransom, Reverdy C. *The Pilgrimage of Harriet Ransom's Son.* Nashville: A.M.E. Sunday School Union, 1950.

Richardson, Harry V. "The Negro in American Religious Life." In *The American Negro Reference Book,* edited by John P. Davis. Englewood Cliffs, N.J.: Prentice-Hall, 1966.

Singleton, George A. *The Romance of African Methodism.* New York: Exposition Press, 1952.

Smith, Kelly Miller. "Religion as a Force in Black America." In *The State of Black America 1982,* edited by James D. Williams. New Brunswick, N.J.: Transaction Books, 1982.

Tanner, C. M. *A Manual of the African Methodist Episcopal Church, Being a Course of Twelve Lectures for Probationers and Members.* Philadelphia: A.M.E. Church Publishing House, 1900.

Thurman, Howard. *The Luminous Darkness: A Personal Interpretation of the Anatomy of Segregation and the Ground of Hope.* New York: Harper & Row, 1965.

———. *The Search for Common Ground.* New York: Harper & Row, 1971.

Tillich, Paul. *Love, Power and Justice.* New York: Oxford University Press, 1960.

———. *Systematic Theology.* Vol. 3. Chicago: University of Chicago Press, 1963.

Tocqueville, Alexis de. *Democracy in America.* Vol. 1. New York: Alfred A. Knopf, 1945.

Walls, William J. *The African Methodist Episcopal Zion Church: Reality of the Black Church.* Charlotte, N.C.: A.M.E. Zion Church Publishing House, 1974.

Washington, Booker T. *Up from Slavery.* In *Three Negro Classics.* New York: Avon Books, 1965.

Washington, Joseph R., Jr. *Black Religion: The Negro and Christianity in the United States*. Boston: Beacon Press, 1964.

Wesley, Charles H. *Richard Allen, Apostle of Freedom*. Washington, D.C.: Associated Publishers, 1935.

Wilmore, Gayraud. *Black Religion and Black Radicalism*. New York: Doubleday & Co., 1972.

————. "Our Heritage and Our Hope." A mimeographed paper delivered and circulated among the members of the Society for the Study of Black Religion at its annual meeting in Jamaica, West Indies, November 1976.

Wilmore, Gayraud S., and Cone, James H., eds. *Black Theology: A Documentary History, 1966–1976*. New York: Orbis Books, 1979.

Wilson, William Julius. *The Declining Significance of Race: Blacks and Changing American Institutions*. Chicago: University of Chicago Press, 1978.

Woodson, Carter G. *History of the Negro Church*. Washington D.C.: Associated Publishers, 1921.

Wright, Nathan, Jr., *Black Power and Urban Unrest*. New York: Hawthorn Books, 1967.

Wright, Bishop R. R. *The Encyclopaedia of the African Methodist Episcopal Church*. 2nd edition. Philadelphia: A.M.E. Church Publishing House, 1947.

AFRICAN METHODIST EPISCOPAL CHURCH QUADRENNIAL MINUTES

Journal of the 20th Quadrennial Session of the General Conference of the A.M.E. Church, held in St. Stephen's A.M.E. Church, Wilmington, N.C., May 4–22, 1896.

Journal of the 23rd Quadrennial Session of the General Conference of the African Methodist Episcopal Church, Norfolk, Va., May 24–31, 1908.

Journal of the 24th Quadrennial Session of the General Conference of the A.M.E. Church, held in Kansas City, Mo., May 6–23, 1912.

Journal of the 30th Quadrennial Session of the African Methodist Episcopal Church, held in New York City, May 6, 1936.

Journal of the 34th Quadrennial Session of the General Conference of the African Methodist Episcopal Church, held in Chicago, Ill., May 1952.

Journal of the 35th Quadrennial Session of the General Conference of the African Methodist Episcopal Church, which convened in Miami, Fla., May, 1956, at the Dinner Key Auditorium.

NATIONAL BAPTIST CONVENTION MINUTES

Journal of the Twentieth Annual Session of the National Baptist Convention held in the Fifth Street Baptist Church, Richmond, Virginia, Sep-

tember 12–17, 1900. Nashville: National Baptist Publishing Board, 1900.

Journal of the 23rd Annual Session of the National Baptist Convention held in Philadelphia, Pennsylvania, September 16–21, 1903.

Journal of the 24th Annual Session of the National Baptist Convention held with the Ebenezer Third Baptist Church, Austin, Texas, September 14–19, 1904. Nashville: National Baptist Publishing Board, 1904.

Journal of the 27th Annual Session of the National Baptist Convention held with the Metropolitan Baptist Church, Washington, D.C., December 11–16, 1907. Nashville: National Baptist Publishing Board, 1908.

Journal of the 29th Annual Session of the National Baptist Convention held with the Baptist Churches of Columbus, Ohio, September 15–20, 1909. Nashville: Baptist Publishing Board, 1910.

Journal of the 31st Annual Session of the National Baptist Convention held with the Baptist churches in Pittsburgh, Pennsylvania, September 13–18th, 1911. Nashville: Sunday School Publishing Board, 1912.

Journal of the 41st Annual Session of the National Baptist Convention, U.S.A., Inc., held with the Baptist churches in New Orleans, Louisiana, 1921. Nashville: National Baptist Publishing Board, 1921.

Journal of the 42nd Annual Session of the National Baptist Convention held with the churches in St. Louis, Missouri, December 6–11, 1922. Nashville: National Baptist Publishing Board, 1923.

Journal of the 50th Annual Session (Jubilee Anniversary) of the National Baptist Convention held with the churches in Chicago, Illinois, August 14–25th, 1930. Nashville: Sunday School Publishing Board, 1931.

Journal of the 55th Annual Session of the National Baptist Convention held with the churches of New York, September 4–9, 1935. Nashville: Sunday School Publishing House, 1936.

Journal of the 60th Annual Session of the National Baptist Convention held with the Baptist churches of Birmingham, Alabama, September 4–9, 1940. Nashville: Sunday School Publishing Board, 1941.

The Record of the 79th Annual Session of the National Baptist Convention, U.S.A., Inc., held with the Baptist churches of San Francisco, California, September 9–13, 1959. Nashville: Sunday School Publishing Board, 1959.

Index

Abolition movement 40, 65, 76, 113

Africa, 28, 35, 59, 79, 83–85

African Methodist Episcopal bishops, 13, 64

African Methodist Episcopal Church, 13, 17, 18, 22 n. 11, 31, 32, 40, 41, 48, 52, 54 nn. 23, 24; 67, 82 n. 15, 92, 96, 107–8

African Methodist Episcopal Zion Church, 22 n. 11, 40, 43, 44, 47, 48, 62, 82 n. 15, 92, 105 n. 8, 115

Allen, Richard (bishop), 17, 18, 19, 40, 41, 54 nn. 22, 23; 55 n. 27

American Colonization Society, 59

Asbury, Francis (bishop), 54 n. 23, 55 n. 27

Black Christianity, 43

Black Christian tradition, 10–20, 24 n. 23, 111, 123, 134

Black Church: and black community, 112; and black theology, 127 n. 22; and Booker T. Washington, 39–40; and civil rights, 71–74; classification, 1–2, 7–8, 20 nn. 1, 2; and its conservative style, 50–52; and W. E. B. DuBois, 39–40; and economics, 69ff.; and education, 67–74; and foreign mission, 79, 87; its ideal societal vision, 45–46, 91, 99, 131; independent, 3, 5–7, 10, 20, 40–43, 49, 85, 109; as institutional center, 8–9, 133; its leadership roles, 66–67; and "liberation," 21 n. 8; and the middle class ethic, 67; its moral aim, 14; and moral conflict, 79–80; and the nation, 107, 116; its oral tradition, 94; its political involvement, 17; and its political thought, 90–98; and power, 114–19; its primary genius, 109; as race institution, 9, 74, 134; and racial development, 67–74, 86; and racism, 116–17; and regional splits, 113; as religious and secular, 8; and reverse racism, 19, 36–37, 40–41; and social change, 58, 64, 74, 90; and social class, 65–67; social and moral development, 64, 74;

153